BEEN THINKING ABOUT

Coming Together Around the
Ideas and Issues that Divide Us

MART DE HAAN

Discovery House Publishers

Books, music, and videos that feed the soul with the Word of God

Box 3566 Grand Rapids, MI 49501

Discovery House Publishers is affiliated with RBC Ministries, Grand Rapids, Michigan.

Discovery House books are distributed to the trade exclusively by Barbour Publishing, Inc., Uhrichsville, Ohio.

Requests for permission to quote from this book should be directed to: Permissions Department, Discovery House Publishers, P.O. Box 3566, Grand Rapids, MI 49501.

Library of Congress Cataloging-in-Publication Data Available on Request

Interior design by Nicholas Richardson

Printed in the United States of America

07 08 09 10 11 12 / BPI / 10 9 8 7 6 5 4 3 2 1

BEEN THINKING ABOUT

Contents

Personalities and Relationships

Beliefs and the Bible

Life in Christ

Gender Issues

Things That Are to Come

FOREWORD

In the mid-1980s, when Mart De Haan was named to the presidency of RBC Ministries, he began writing a monthly column of ideas and opinions called Been Thinking About. Over the years, a growing number of people have come to appreciate the honest and balanced approach to Scripture that characterize Mart's thinking.

Now, Discovery House Publishers is pleased to offer a selection of these columns in book form for the first time. We hope you'll find help for your own spiritual journey in these thoughtful writings. As you look at the topics and dip into those that catch your interest, you'll discover careful treatment of Scripture, personal vulnerability, respect for divergent opinions, and familiar concepts expressed in fresh ways. Walk awhile with Mart as he examines tough topics in a reflective way and gently challenges you to think through some of the difficult issues that can polarize followers of Christ. Enjoy the journey!

—The Publisher

God and His Ways

IMPONDERABLES

WHERE DID GOD COME FROM?

Could a creator who made the earth out of nothing come from nowhere? Even a lowly mosquito doesn't just happen without a spawning pond or puddle.

Don't get me wrong. I'm a believer. I see the logic of believing in a first cause great enough and personal enough to explain everything that exists. But when it comes to the origin of such a Person, who can figure?

That's not all. What was this God doing for the eternity before us? How will He keep us satisfied and challenged in an endless future? Why would He make billions of people that He knew were going to reject Him?

Who, while trying to understand the existence or ways of God, hasn't felt their mind shudder like a car driven beyond its limits? Who, while trying to absorb the meaning of an eternal, uncaused, first cause, hasn't found their sanity tested by the thought of a never-ending past and future?

One reason for asking these imponderable questions is that such riddles bring us not only to the end of ourselves, but to the beginning of a new understanding of God. From the first words of Genesis, we are introduced to a God who makes no effort to answer all of our questions. Instead He gradually leads us to conclude that only when we have exhausted the limits of our own reason can we learn to trust the One who asks, "To whom then will you liken Me, or to whom shall I be equal?" (Isaiah 40:25).

This is not to say that belief in God depends on an escape from reason. Spiritual insight is not found by emptying our minds of questions. According to the Book of books, spiritual renewal follows the invitation, "'Come now, and let us reason together,' says the LORD" (Isaiah 1:18). In the pages that follow, the prophet Isaiah goes on to quote a God who appeals to the minds and thoughts of His people. Over and over the God of the Bible asks His people to do their best thinking and to trust Him for answers that He alone understands.

Only after appealing to the highest reason and best judgment of His hearers does the prophet go on to ask, "Have you not known? Have you not heard? The everlasting God, the LORD, the Creator of the ends of the earth, neither faints nor is weary. His understanding is unsearchable. He gives power to the weak, and to those who have no might He increases strength. Even the youths shall faint and be weary, and the young men shall utterly fall, but those who wait on the LORD shall renew their strength; they shall mount up with wings like eagles, they shall run and not be weary, they shall walk and not faint (Isaiah 40:28–31).

When read in context, Isaiah's invitation to acknowledge the imponderable nature and existence of God is not a call to empty our minds and embrace the irrational. Rather his challenge is to use our best thinking to put ourselves at the mercy and service of the One who has left His signature and fingerprints all over our world and lives.

Lesser gods do not give us reason to rest in the presence of questions we cannot answer. When we have mastered them, smaller gods, like good jobs or bank accounts, replace our desire to have with a fear of losing. Little gods, made in our own image, are all imposters and liars. They rob our strength without renewing it. This is the mindless legacy of the idols we carve for ourselves in the presence of our Creator (Isaiah 40:18–25).

In this "information age" it's important for us to be reminded of the limitations of our own understanding. Faced with the phenomenal growth of the Internet and the explosion of information services, we could be tempted to think that, in time, an exploding technology will unravel the problems and imponderables of life. We might forget the wisdom of Moses who wrote, "The secret things belong to the LORD our God, but those things which are revealed belong to us and to our children forever, that we may do all the words of this law" (Deuteronomy 29:29).

For some of us, the World Wide Web has become a substitute for the Word of God. The worship of information has become in some ways like a modern "tower of Babel" (Genesis 11:6). With a vision of "global access to all knowledge" humanity is hoping, through shared knowledge, to solve the ultimate problems of aging, birth defects, disease, and mortality. Once again we are tempted like our first parents to trade trust for the pursuit of knowledge that is beyond our ability to manage.

Yet, there is another option. After we have done our best thinking, we could choose to be like the family dog who sleeps peacefully at our feet. Dakota, Doc, and Dutchess aren't known as "man's best friends" for being foolish. Admittedly they don't know what we know. They don't understand our reasons, dreams, or concerns. They don't even care where we get the money to buy their food. But they do know us. They sense when we drive in the driveway at the end of the day. They greet us at the door and are willing to rest at our feet while our minds go places they have never imagined. They trust us for some of the same reasons we can trust our own Master and provider.

Father in heaven, You deserve so much more than we have given You. We know that our problem is not that we cannot understand You. Our sin is that we have no good excuse when we hear You say, "Hear, O heavens, and give ear, O earth! For the LORD has spoken: 'I have nourished and brought up children, and they have rebelled against Me; the ox knows its owner and the donkey its master's crib; but Israel does not know, My people do not consider" (Isaiah 1:2–3).

Forgive us for thinking that we cannot trust what we do not fully understand.

October 2005

THE EXISTENCE OF GOD

A MATURE CHRISTIAN woman recently told me of an experience that caused her to doubt the existence of God.

Hearing a woman of the church talk about her doubts got my attention. Over the years I've thought of women not only as the gender chosen to give physical birth but most likely to nurture spiritual life as well.

By contrast, I know men who resonate with a line from *Inherit the Wind*, the dramatic portrayal of the famous Scopes Monkey Trial. The event was historic. The state was challenging a teacher's right to teach evolution in public schools. When a prospective juror was being examined for religious prejudice, he replied, "My wife tends to religion for both of us." His comment reminds me of Paul's New Testament letter to Timothy where he refers to the faith that was first in Timothy's grandmother and mother (2 Timothy 1:5). Over the years I've known many women who have faithfully prayed for their unbelieving children, husbands, and fathers.

Yet after the recent conversation, I began to think about the wives and mothers I've known who, at difficult times in their lives, have had deep and disturbing questions about the existence of God. And I remembered the obvious—that neither men nor women are immune to crises of faith.

Reasons to Doubt

I suspect that women experience spiritual uncertainty for many of the same reasons men do. Global disasters, personal losses, unanswered prayers, church scandals, and abuse of spiritual authority are just some of the factors that can cause both men and women to wonder if their faith in God has been wishful thinking.

An additional complication for people of the church is the pressure we feel to deny our doubts. While agnostics and atheists use unanswerable questions to support their worldview, it is more difficult for people of faith to face and process thoughts that seem to threaten what is most important to us. Other resistance comes from friends and family who are alarmed by tough and irreverent questions. Then there is the pressure that seems to come from the Bible itself. What are we supposed to think when the first words of Genesis simply say, "In the beginning God created the heavens and the earth"?

How can we turn our minds off and just assume that God is there? How can we "just believe" in One who has always existed? Why would there be a God in the first place? In the shadows of such looming questions, it's important for us to know that Moses wasn't asking for a blind leap when he wrote the first words of Genesis.

Reasons to Believe

Imagine looking over Moses' shoulder as he slowly pens, "In the beginning, God created the heavens and the earth." What could he have been thinking? What reasons did he have to believe? What did he know about his subject as he wrote his famous opening line?

Exodus came before Genesis: Since Moses was born long after Adam and Eve, we know he was not sitting on a rock watching creation happen when he wrote Genesis. So where was he? The only plausible answer I'm aware of is that he compiled the book of beginnings while camped in the Wilderness of Sinai—*after* the supernatural events of the Exodus.

The miracles that broke the grip of the Egyptian pharaoh were part of the national record by the time Moses started writing. With millions of his countrymen, he had seen a powerful God open a path through the Red Sea and defeat the armies of Egypt. Together they had seen Him provide for their hungry, thirsty children in a barren, sun-baked wilderness. Day after day, they had seen God's presence in a pillar of smoke by day, and fire by night. Camped at the foot of Mount Sinai, they had heard His voice. Then, in some of the darkest and most memorable days of their lives, they had seen a plague swallow up members of the families who had not learned to fear or trust the God who had been revealing Himself to them.

Moses' knowledge of God was more than wishful thinking or speculative philosophy. It was a compelling fact of history. The powerful, undeniable evidence he saw left no doubts in his mind that there was a God who cared for him and the people he led.

Christ came before the church: The practice of using history to confirm the existence and love of God is repeated throughout the Bible. Many years after Moses, a woman named Mary of Magdala spread the word that she had seen Jesus of Nazareth after His resurrection from the dead (John 20:18). Later, the rest of Jesus' disciples joined her in confirming not only His empty grave, but face-to-face meetings with Him after His execution and burial. In one of these meetings, a man named Thomas touched Jesus' scarred body while the other disciples looked on. In another meeting on the shore of Galilee, Jesus prepared a fish breakfast and ate with a group of His friends.

The God who proved Himself to Israel by making "the exodus" part of their national history is the One who gave the church a "new exodus" through the life, death, and resurrection of Christ. As God used Moses to lead Israel out of slavery in Egypt, He used His Son to lead His people out of the greater bondage of sin and death.

Although many questions remain, one answer is clear. The God of the exodus and the resurrection doesn't expect us to just believe in Him. In addition to the historical record of the Bible, He has left His fingerprints and signature all over creation (Romans 1:18–21), and His footprints in the circumstances of our lives (Acts 17:22–34).

Father in heaven, thank You for giving us the national record of Your people and the life, death, and resurrection of Your Son. Thank You for showing us not only that You exist but that You care for us with a love that is so much greater than our doubts.

DOES GOD PLAY FAVORITES?

WHY WOULD A PARENT DO more for some of his children than for others? Why does our Father in heaven seem to repeat the mistake of a well-known biblical patriarch? Jacob provoked family rivalry among his twelve sons by spoiling young Joseph in the presence of his older brothers (Genesis 37:3).

So often our Father seems to do more for new believers than for those of us who have been around for a while. Recent converts often tell stories of dramatic answers to prayer, even as those of us who have been in the family for a long time struggle under the weight of problems our Father could have lifted from our backs long ago.

Why does a Father of unlimited resources seem tight-fisted with some of His children while being so open-handed with others? And why does a Father who is everywhere at all times seem to withdraw from some while walking so closely with others? Is God like a parent who creates havoc in the family by playing favorites?

I'm convinced that answers to these questions can be found in a case study of the children of Israel. In the developmental phases of their national life, God the Father showed that He relates differently to newborns than to adolescent and adult children.

An Infant Needs Direct Help to Survive

When the Father of Israel delivered His newborn nation from the bricks and whips of Egypt, He did so with great style. With the fireworks of a great storm exploding in the Egyptian sky, and with the persuasion of mounting plagues, God tightened His grip on the throat of the pharaoh until the self-proclaimed sovereign of Egypt choked and slumped, gasping in grief and angry defeat.

Just as God gave the infant children of Israel this impressive display of His power, He often welcomes newborn believers into His family with a clear and present sense of deliverance from their sin. He may give them real and vivid experiences to show He is a God who is everything His children need Him to be.

New believers at this stage often give encouragement to the whole family of God as they describe with fresh awareness and enthusiasm what God has done for them. In telling of their experiences, however, they are not yet aware that ahead of them are mountains to scale, swamps to wade, and seasons to endure.

A Young Child Needs to Learn Boundaries

As the children of Israel walked out of Egypt they breathed free air for the first time in centuries. There were no whips cracking at their backs. No fences to confine them. No crops to plant. Their food was delivered daily. Water gushed out of rocks. The sky was big over their heads. The ground was wide under their feet. The possibilities of the future seemed unlimited.

Then came a change. At the foot of Mount Sinai, God gave His children rules. In time someone would count these rules. There were 613 in all: 365 negative commands like "don't ignore the plight of an overloaded animal"; 248 positive commands like "return lost property to its owner."

The school of Sinai represents the line upon line of education that is needed by all children. The God who miraculously rescued His children from bondage then teaches us the principles of freedom. With the benefits of relationship come the boundaries of family rules.

At first the rules seem overwhelming. Do this. Don't do that. No. You're going to get hurt. Ouch! That's why Mom and Dad warned you! Slowly the period of God's supernatural intervention is eclipsed by a new period of learning. As God provides for us, He wants us to learn that trust is not just a passive experience. Trusting Him on His terms means being willing to do what He tells us to do. The struggle begins.

An Adolescent Needs to Learn Self-Control

Forty years later, the children of Israel stood at the threshold of the Promised Land. After years of preparation in the presence of God, they were ready to move into their own homes. As they stepped into that new land, the miracle of food from heaven stopped. Instead of living under the obvious evidence of God's protective shadow, they would have to plant their own crops, cultivate the soil, pull weeds, and prayerfully wait upon God for the early and latter rains. God was teaching them a new form of trust. Now His miracles, though just as real, and while just as many, would be hidden behind the curtain of unpredictable weather and natural problems.

Gradually and lovingly our supernatural God teaches us the disciplines of trust in ways that give us a chance to live by faith rather than by sight.

An Adult Child Needs to Learn the Independent Side of Dependence

In the centuries that followed, God remained present with His people. On occasion He would give them dramatic miracles of provision. As a rule, however, the wonder of His presence and provisions were clothed in the natural cause-and-effect relationships of life. He still provided daily for His people, but He did so in increasingly subtle ways.

Sometimes we become confused by the apparent absence of God in our lives. But honest reflection will show us that God is absent only in the sense that He is not giving us everything we want when we want it. He still provides for us constantly or we would not survive the need for another breath. But like a seasoned coach, a loving parent, and a wise teacher, He has gradually given us the impression that we are on our own. Does He do this so we will have to provide for ourselves? No. He does it so our trust in Him will grow, not diminish.

Lord, forgive us for demanding the ways and days of our childhood. Forgive us for wondering if You care for us less now than when You were holding our hand more tightly and obviously than You are today. Thank You for being with us in the dark of night, even when we seem so alone. Thank You for being so patient with us, and for leading us in a way that gives us an opportunity to trust You more rather than less.

February 2000

THE GIFT

IMAGINE FILLING OUT AN application for heaven. After filling in your name and address, you come to a section marked "Qualifications." What would you put there? "My belief in God"? "The people I have helped along the way"? "I've tried to live by the Ten Commandments"? Or would you write, "No qualifications other than my reliance upon what Christ, the Son of God, has done for me"? The reason these questions are important is that if we treat salvation as a reward rather than a gift, we may fail to qualify for the gift. Out of concern for those who could be missing the opportunity of a lifetime, I'd like to suggest ten reasons to believe salvation is a gift:

1. The Bible calls it a gift.

According to the most published book in the world, no one qualifies for heaven by trying to be a good person (Romans 4:4–5; 6:23; 10:13). Nor will we live forever because we have done better than our neighbor. According to the Bible, the only way to live forever is through a willingness to receive "the gift of God" (Ephesians 2:7–9).

2. There are risks in receiving it.

Those who receive gifts often feel beholden to the giver. This sense of moral obligation is true of those who receive God's offer of salvation. According to the apostle Paul in the New Testament, such persons are no longer their own. They've been "bought at a price" (1 Corinthians 6:19–20). While a sense of moral responsibility does not always accompany a gift, it often is felt by those who know they've been given something they didn't earn.

3. It is offered by grace.

The apostle Paul said, "By grace you have been saved" (Ephesians 2:8). "By grace" means the "unmerited kindness" by which God offers to rescue us from our failures. This help comes only to those who have given up hope of qualifying for heaven by their own accomplishments or by comparing themselves with others. The apostles James and Peter both called attention to a foundational principle of the kingdom of God when they said, "God resists the proud, but gives grace to the humble" (James 4:6; 1 Peter 5:5).

4. It is received through faith.

If the Bible only said, "By grace you have been saved," we might conclude that everyone will receive eternal life. Without the added condition of faith, it would appear that everyone, whether atheist or apostle, will end up with the gift we don't deserve. The complete statement, however, says, "By grace you have been saved through faith." We need this faith in order to qualify for the gift (Romans 1:16–17; 4:4–5). Unless we see that salvation is received only by trusting what God has done for us, we are still relying on ourselves.

5. The most undeserving people can receive it.

The Bible gives us the names of people whose only quali-
fication for heaven was that they believed in God's provision
for their rescue. These examples include a prostitute named
Rahab, a despised tax collector named Matthew, and a demon-
possessed woman named Mary of Magdala. Then there was the
criminal who was executed at the side of Christ. Only because
salvation is a gift could Jesus say to him, "Today you will be
with Me in Paradise" (Luke 23:39–43).

6. It was paid for by another.

From the beginning of time, God used the sacrifice of
innocent animals to show that a person's wrongs could be paid
for by a sinless substitute. Even though the blood of animals
could not pay for human sin, God used these sacrifices to
foreshadow an event that became the center page of human
history. At the appointed time, the sinless Son of God gave
His life in our behalf. Then He rose from the dead, which
proved that God had accepted His death as payment for our sin
(1 Corinthians 15:1–8).

7. It was wrapped with care.

In fulfillment of God's plan that was made before the creation of the world (Ephesians 1:3–7), the gift of salvation
was packaged in the colorful ritual of temple sacrifice. Later
it was wrapped in the predictions of prophets who promised
that God's "Anointed One" would die for our sin (Isaiah 53;
Daniel 9:24–26). At just the right time, the present of heaven
was placed in the body of a young woman and wrapped in the
flesh of a tiny Jewish baby.

8. There are strings attached.

Those who accept a gift have a moral obligation to appreciate the value of what has been given them. This sense of duty was evident in the apostle Paul. After receiving salvation in Christ he longed to impart to his readers in Rome "some spiritual gift" (Romans 1:11). He went on to say that he owed something to everyone who had not yet heard about what God had done for them (Romans 1:14–17). As Paul had received freely from God, he sensed his obligation to freely give.

9. There is a precedent.

From beginning to end, our life depends on a series of gifts. First, God gave us the gift of existence. Then He gave us the provisions and circumstances we need to survive. He gave us the ability to see, to feel, to hear, and to enjoy. In light of these gifts, the apostle Paul asked, "Who makes you differ from another? And what do you have that you did not receive? Now if you did indeed receive it, why do you boast as if you had not received it?" (1 Corinthians 4:7).

10. A gift is what we need.

This is the most personal reason for believing salvation is a gift. If the Bible is telling us the truth about ourselves, we don't need fairness and justice. Neither do we need compensation or rewards. We need mercy. We need forgiveness. We need to open our hearts to the undeserved rescue God gives to anyone who receives the ultimate gift of relationship with His Son (John 1:11–12).

Father in heaven, thank You for doing for us what we could never do for ourselves. We gratefully acknowledge that because of Your gift, we are not only Yours by creation but by Your purchase as well.

December 2000

THE PEOPLE VS. JOB

PUBLIC INTEREST IN high-profile court cases often declines once the outcome is known.

The People vs. Job, however, is a landmark decision that never loses its significance. In one of the most published trials in history we see the eyes of heaven and hell focused on earth. In the same public record we see mirrored our own inclination to play judge and jury with one another's lives.

Summary of the Trial

A self-declared advocate of the human race files a class-action suit against God. According to a prosecutor from hell, the Lord of heaven has resorted to bribery. The opening arguments of Satan allege that God has bought the loyalty of a man who has remained faithful to his Creator.

As the accuser sees it, Job is no fool. He is the pride of heaven only because he is on the take. He remains faithful because God has built fences of protection around his family, his health, and a business to brag about.

In response to the indictment, God allows the accuser to test Job's motives with a series of personal losses. Within days, Job loses what others spend their whole lives trying to get and protect. But what drives Job beyond grief to madness is the testimony of three friends who side with the prosecution in attacking his character. Each of them insists that Job is denying the scandal that would explain his suffering. In a series of arguments that escalate in eloquence and anger, Job and friends insult and alienate one another until the Lord of heaven breaks His silence. With a surprise move, God brings the trial to an end with a compelling exhibit of physical evidence.

Let's take a closer look at why Job's story has become a timeless case study for people who are trying to make sense of their own troubles, and of the God in heaven who is allowing them to suffer.

Who is Job?

From the details of the story, God's co-defendant is probably a contemporary of Abraham, the richest man in the East (Job 1:3), and a friend of the poor. No stranger to legal proceedings, Job defends the cause of widows and orphans until the day he finds himself in the middle of his own trial (Job 29–31).

What are his friends thinking?

Three of Job's friends think they know why he is suffering. They are convinced that "you reap what you sow" in life, and back one another up in arguing for a direct correlation between Job's losses and some secret, moral failure he is refusing to admit (Job 4:7–8). Over and over they press the same logic. God doesn't make mistakes. When we suffer, we are getting a return on the bad seed we have planted.

Actually, Job's friends are theologically correct in much of what they say. They know God doesn't punish good and reward evil. But when they try to defend God against Job's complaint of unfairness, they unwittingly become witnesses for the prosecution. Lacking heaven's perspective, they argue that their friend must be suffering in proportion to a sin he is hiding.

Has God Forgotten Him?

Job's answer to this question is surprising. Instead of saying, "My God, my God, why have You forsaken me?" he says, in effect, "My God, my God, why won't You leave me alone?" Rather than thinking that heaven is ignoring his agony, he sighs and gasps, "What is man that you make so much of him, that you give him so much attention, that you examine him every morning and test him every moment? Will you never look away from me, or let me alone even for an instant? If I have sinned, what have I done to you, O watcher of men? Why have you made me your target? Have I become a burden to you?" (Job 7:17–20 NIV).

What Job does not understand is that the court has declared as inadmissible evidence a prior conversation between God and Satan that would explain his suffering.

A Surprise Ending

When God finally speaks, He doesn't tell Job why He let him suffer. Neither does He blame Satan for what happened. The Lord of heaven doesn't even thank the three friends for trying to defend the honor of the Almighty.

Instead, in a surprise move, He calls His co-defendant to the witness stand and asks Job questions like, "Where were you when I created the world? Can you understand how I did it? Can you do what I've done?" Then God talks about the weather, the ever-changing wind, and clouds that gather waters and then release them on command. With closing arguments that seem to come from nowhere, and then from everywhere, the great Judge of the universe presents a compelling series of physical exhibits.

The implication is clear: "If I am powerful and wise enough to create Orion in the night sky, a wild ox, and an ostrich, can you trust Me in the trouble I have allowed into your life?"

Job's complaints are silenced. The indictment of his accusers is overturned. The witness of the natural world to the immeasurable wisdom and power of God is enough to bring Job to his knees and to his senses.

And now as we are tested, an eagle soars overhead. A tree pushes roots deep into rich earth while lifting its branches to the sun. A wolf howls. Sheep wander around looking for grass. A full moon lights the night. And The People vs. Job waits to be remembered.

Father in heaven, we see ourselves in Job's trial. Like the devil who accused him, we look at those who love You more than we do and assume that they are on the take. Like the three friends who sided with his accuser, we look at those who are doing worse than we are and assume that they are suffering in proportion to their sin. And sometimes, even in small troubles, we are like Job himself. We get so confused, and so angry. We exhaust ourselves with demands for You to show yourself, until—with Job, we slump in quiet worship before the witness of what You have already done for us, and in us, and around us.

September 2005

TRUST

DOES OUR LORD TRUST US? How could He? He tells us not to trust ourselves (Proverbs 3:5–7). For our own sake He urges us not to trust in our own knowledge, strength, relationships, or accomplishments. Nor are we to trust in one another (Psalm 118:8).

Our confidence is to be in Him alone.

Yet there is another side of the coin. The Scriptures make it clear that while God does not want us to trust ourselves, He does want us to entrust ourselves to one another as an expression of our confidence in Him (Proverbs 24:6; 2 Timothy 2:2; 1 Corinthians 12:13–27).

Even more important is what God Himself entrusts to us. He gives students to teachers, citizens to presidents, children to parents, church members to pastors, and workers to employers. He entrusts wives to husbands, neighbors to neighbors, and friends to friends.

Yet there is more. He has also given the earth to man, the gospel to His church, and His own name to all who have accepted His Son as their own personal Savior.

Together the gifts of God reflect the extent of our steward-ship (1 Corinthians 4:1–2; Luke 19:11–27). Stewardship is the responsibility of caring for that which belongs to another. Such oversight is what the Bible has in view when it tells us about the gifts God has given to His people to be used for His honor. As a rule we think of these gifts as the good things God gives: money, abilities, life, time, health, relationships. These good gifts we know are entrusted to His people to be used for His purposes (James 1:5–20).

Yet there is more that God gives us. He also entrusts His people with pain and disappointment. In difficult and trouble-some times our Lord places in our care the kind of loss that gives us another way to show His supernatural presence in our lives.

The uncomfortable truth is that while good circumstances can be received and enjoyed to the honor of God, it is more likely that God's grace will be noticed in those who trust Him in the middle of disappointment and hardship (2 Corinthians 4:7–11).

The apostle Paul would not have had a chance to make such a powerful statement with his life if he had been entrusted with only rich and comfortable circumstances. But because he fol-lowed Christ not only in moments of material affluence but also in many kinds of suffering and personal hardship, his losses help us define the potential of well-grounded faith and love. When we read of Paul's willingness to endure separation from family and friends, shipwreck, stonings, beatings, and repeated whippings with thirty-nine lashes, we can be sure that he was not in the ministry for self-serving reasons. On many occasions he suffered a lack of clothing, food, strength, and health. On a daily basis he bore concern over the spiritual well-being of the people and churches he loved (2 Corinthians 4:7–12; 11:23–33).

Paul was entrusted with all of this pain. Through many difficulties, he showed his faith in the resurrected Christ. Through his weakness, and the resulting experience of the strength of God, every succeeding generation has been spiritually enriched (Philippians 4:11–13).

So too, Job was entrusted with pain and loss. Sarah and Hannah were given the tears of childlessness. Then there was Joseph. From a pit in Israel to a prison in Egypt, he used false accusations and imprisonment to show the world that God is in the shadows even in the darkest moments of our lives.

Does God trust us with such pain? No. He knows our inclinations. He knows that left to ourselves we would be unprofitable servants. Allowed to go our own way we are apt to let our disappointments result in bitterness and prayerlessness. Yet with a promise to never leave us, He entrusts us with challenges that give us a chance to trust Him in our tears as well as in our laughter.

Never can we bear the weight of what has been entrusted to us in our own strength. When we try, we crumble in defeat. Only by throwing ourselves on Him and only by trusting in His mercy and ability to save can we see the worst mistakes and problems turned around for the honor of God and for the good of all who come in contact with us.

Father, thank You for entrusting to us what only You by Your Spirit can protect. Please accept our willingness and yieldedness as an invitation to turn our disappointments as well as our good times into a lasting memorial to You.

October 1998

SNOOPY

For FIFTY YEARS cartoonist Charles Schulz gave us pictures of ourselves wrapped in a smile. One of the last strips I clipped from our Sunday paper showed Snoopy the dog sitting on top of his doghouse with a typewriter, writing about his life. He titled his story . . .

The Dog Who Never Did Anything

Snoopy remembers it this way: "You stay home now," they said, "and be a good dog."

So he stayed home and was a good dog.

Then he decided to be even a better dog. So he barked at everyone who went by. And he even chased the neighbor's cats.

"What's happened to you?" they said. "You used to be such a good dog."

So he stopped barking and chasing cats, and everyone said, "You're a good dog."

The moral, as Snoopy typed it, is: "Don't do anything and you'll be a good dog."

As I turned the smile around in my mind, I noticed a quirk of the English language. Snoopy and God have something in common. They are related not only by alphabet (dog and god), but by what "creatures in the middle" expect of them. The idea intrigued me enough to try another version.

The God Who Never Did Anything

"You give me what I want now," they said, "and be a good God."

So He gave them what they wanted and He was a good God.

Then He decided to be an even better God.

He started knocking over the furniture of other gods, and He used pain to help people in ways they could not understand.

"What's happened to You?" they said. "You used to be such a good God."

So He stopped knocking over the furniture of other gods, and He stopped using pain in ways that were beyond people's ability to understand.

And everyone said, "You're a good God."

The moral, as angels might see it: "Stop acting like God and people will think You're good."

The God We Want

Many of us imagine God as we want Him to be. To our wishes we add expectation. We expect Him to encourage us when we are afraid, to comfort us when we're hurt, to forgive us when we fail, and to give us what we think we need when we think we need it.

Yet, along the way, we keep stumbling into the awareness that the King of Heaven is more apt to come to us in His own style, time, and mystery. He is seldom as we imagine Him to be. He is more like the God who reveals Himself in the pages of His own history. There He comes to us in the unexpected surprises of joy, in the unwanted nights of our misery, and in the solitary sounds of our own loneliness. He comes to us in the unexpected joys of Adam, in the numbed grief of Eve, in the inconsolable tears of the childless Hannah, in the murderous anger of Moses, and in the madness of a powerful Nebuchadnezzar.

But me? Until He responds, I'd rather have it my way. In the moments of my dissatisfaction, I don't want to have to wait for what I want. I want it now. Now. I'll pray. I'll pay. I'll bargain. I'll crawl on my knees. But I want God to prove that He is good—right now.

The God Who Has Been Good

Even in our "maturity" we can be like two- and three-year-olds pulling at the pant leg of heaven. Our Father isn't surprised. He knows how to raise physical, emotional, and spiritual toddlers. He knows how to run with us in our youth, and how to walk with us at seventy-four, eighty-four, and ninety-four.

And for those who go further, He is still there, hearing once again our whimpers in the night, and reaching down with the affection of an adoring mother who carefully lifts her children from their crib to herself.

No, He has not always been the kind of parent we wanted Him to be. Yes, He has been good on His terms rather than on ours. He has not answered our prayers in the way we asked. Seldom has He allowed anything to play out according to our own expectations or childish demands. Yet His determination to lead us in the paths of His own choosing is what has made Him so good.

The God Who Will Be Good

The promise of tomorrow comes with the wrinkled snap-shots of yesterday. Even though our memories are not as sharp as we'd like them to be, and even though the happy times are mixed with regret, our albums contain memories of a God who keeps reminding us that He is better than our expectations. He is better than our demands. He is better than anything this life has to offer.

If He allowed a relationship to be lost, He stayed with us to remind us that we weren't made for one another as much as we were made for Him. As our bodies give way to time, they become painful reminders that we were not made for these bodies. We were made for the One who said from the top of a thundering, burning mountain—to a people huddled in the middle of a life-threatening wilderness—"I am the Lord your God, who brought you out of the land of Egypt, out of the house of bondage. You shall have no other gods before Me."

This is the God who, because He is good, refuses to "stay home and do nothing."

Father, thank You for a man named Charles Schulz who brought us elements of truth amid our smiles. Thank You for being God on Your terms rather than ours. May Your name be hallowed as we wait on You. May Your kingdom be reflected in our patience. May Your will be done in our disappointments. Please, give us this day our daily bread.

August 2004

THE DAY GOD DIED

ON APRIL 8, 1966, THE cover of *Time* magazine asked in bold black letters, "Is God Dead?" The lead story described the work of several theologians who no longer held to traditional concepts of God. They were alike in concluding that the God of our fathers had not survived the dawn of evolution and birth control.

The debate that followed wasn't as much about God as it was about us. We were in the middle of a turbulent decade. Our world was changing. An unpopular war in Vietnam was prompting bumper stickers that said, "Question Authority." Science and technology were improving our lives and making us less aware of our need for a supernatural God.

Other Reasons to Believe God Is Dead

Challenges to the traditional view of God multiplied in the decades that followed. Not all were secular. Consumer fraud in religious broadcasting subjected the God of the Bible to public ridicule. Promises of "blessings for dollars" associated the name of Christ with "get rich quick" or "get thin fast" scams.

Most recently, evidence of clergy abuse surfaced in the public media. With these reports came stories of victims, who, because of their abuse, no longer considered the God of the church a live option.

Those enlightened by science or disillusioned by religious leaders, however, are not the only ones talking about the death of God.

The Bible Also Talks About the Death of God

The God of the Bible was so deeply moved by the harm people do to one another that He actually *died* because of it. At a moment in time, the eternal God closed His eyes and stopped breathing. Under the weight of wrongs that had hurt those who were dear to Him, His body fell limp and lifeless. At that moment God was dead—not just in the perception of others, but in real time and in an actual place.

In making this claim, the Bible goes far beyond the cover and pages of *Time* magazine. Instead of asking, "Is God Dead?" the theology of the Bible leaves us with a mystery that is beyond human comprehension (1 Timothy 3:16). The Second Person of a three-in-one God became a real man to die a real death for us (Philippians 2:5–11; John 1:1–3, 14).

As this unparalleled drama unfolds, physical death was not our God's greatest sacrifice. Even before breathing His final breath on a Roman cross, He endured the hellish darkness of spiritual separation from His Father in heaven. As the skies darkened in the middle of the day, His anguished cry echoed through the halls of heaven and history: "My God, My God, why have You forsaken Me?" (Matthew 27:46).

According to the Bible, our Creator endured such an agonizing death to show us that He is alive and that He loves us.

What the Death of God Tells Us About Ourselves

Those of us who are inclined to think of ourselves as victims, rather than offenders, might conclude that Christ's death probably says more about the evil of others than about ourselves. We can always point to someone we think gave us an excuse to respond in an unloving way.

We get a different picture, however, when we look more closely into the suffering of Christ. If the Bible is right, He didn't die just for someone else's sins. He died for *us* (Romans 5:8; John 3:16). The pain He endured says volumes about the extreme nature of our *own* need (Romans 3:10–20).

Anyone who wants to be included in Christ's death must admit that in God's eyes our *own* wrongs rise to the level of those who violate federal law with capital offenses. The extent of His sacrifice says that without His intervention *we* would still be condemned lawbreakers, without hope, and waiting on "death row" for what the Bible calls "the second death" (Revelation 20:14; Romans 6:23).

How the Death of God Can Help Us Find a New Life

The Scriptures offer no hope to those who refuse to believe Christ suffered for them. The Bible offers a whole new life, however, to those who believe that Christ lived and died as their substitute. Like persons who enter a witness protection program, those who find refuge in Christ take on a new identity. Their troubled past is hidden in Him (Colossians 3:3). They assume His name. They receive His Spirit and become temples of the living God (1 Corinthians 3:16; 6:19).

Those who allow the Spirit of Christ to be seen in them are an antidote to the opinion that "God Is Dead." Their happiness and tears become a quiet showcase for the love, and joy, and peace of a God who is alive and reaching out to others through

His people. No one does this perfectly. But few things are needed more than imperfect, troubled, grateful people who are growing in their willingness to let Christ live His life through them (Romans 8:11).

How can we come to that surrender? We can begin by watching Jesus our Lord move through the Garden of Gethsemane to the center page of human history. On the way He groans, "Nevertheless, not My will but Yours be done." Then in the middle of a howling mob, on a hill outside the walls of Jerusalem, He willingly endured the eternal weight of our sin and death—for us.

Father in heaven, we never want to stop thanking You for the price You paid for us. Yet we are so easily distracted. Please help us this day to renew our gratitude for Your Son's death. Please use the surrender of this moment to let His life, and Yours, be seen in us today.

April 2003

THE CREATIVE PROCESS

TEACHERS OF CREATIVE THINKING sometimes say, "All things are connected. Try to find relationships where you've never seen them before."

The exercise might raise questions among those who are more committed to "living by the book" than to "thinking outside the box." On the other hand, it could be that no one has a better reason to believe "all things are connected" than those who take the Bible seriously.

Let me give you an example. You decide whether you think "the connection" is real or imagined.

Could there be a parallel between the creative process God used to make the earth and the process He now wants to use to reorder our inner world? The case sounds like this.

The God who created the earth made something out of nothing. He brought order out of chaos and spoke light into the darkness.

Thousands of years later, this same Creator is still speaking light into the darkness. Now, however, He is speaking into a world of darkened hearts that, for many generations, have been turning their backs on Him (John 1:1–14). The God who now wants to re-create our inner world comes with the assurance that, in Christ, He gives us everything we need (2 Peter 1:1–4).

Thus, Peter, a close friend and apostle of Christ, writes, "For this very reason, giving all diligence, add to your faith virtue, to virtue knowledge, to knowledge self-control, to self-control perseverance, to perseverance godliness, to godliness brotherly kindness, and to brotherly kindness love. For if these things are yours and abound, you will be neither barren nor unfruitful in the knowledge of our Lord Jesus Christ" (2 Peter 1:5–8).

Now see if you hear echoes of Genesis in the connections Peter calls for.

The Spirit of God Moved Upon the Waters

In your faith, virtue—Faith works in the darkness of what we cannot see. Virtue, in turn, involves a desire for moral excellence that has its origin in God. When the whole earth was dark and under water, the Spirit of God moved to replace the chaos with something good. Today, in our own darkness and confusion, God asks us to open our minds to a goodness that is better than anything we can presently see or imagine.

Let There Be Light

In virtue, knowledge—When our hearts are ready for a new vision of goodness, Peter urges us to pursue knowledge. In context it is clear that he is referring to knowledge that has its source in Christ (vv. 1–3). His counsel resonates with the insight of another apostle who wrote, "The God who commanded light to shine out of darkness, . . . has shone in our hearts to give the light of the knowledge of the glory of God in the face of Jesus Christ" (2 Corinthians 4:6).

Even if we cannot see into the darkness around us, the understanding we need to renew our thinking about God and others is found in the grace and truth of Christ.

Let There Be Boundaries

In knowledge, self-control—In this context, self-control means to "hold in check" the natural desires that could otherwise control and consume us. In view are those self-centered urges that, if not "held back," would leave no room for the good God wants to do in us. Peter's counsel is in step with the first creation. After speaking light into the darkness, our Creator set boundaries for air, land, and sea. He separated the waters below from the clouds above. Then He held back the oceans to form sandy beaches and rocky coastlines. By a similar process He now calls for inner boundaries that will make room for the new thoughts and ways He is giving us.

Let There Be Seasons

In self-control, perseverance—As God-given self-control enables us to "hold in" natural desire, patience makes it possible to "hold up" under the weight of ever-changing circumstances. Spirit-enabled perseverance, or endurance, allows God's plan to unfold in His time. New ways of thinking form and deepen in the steadfast confidence that God will keep His promises. Here again there are echoes of the first creation. The God of eternity knew how much time He would use to do His work. By designing a complex, sustainable food chain, He anticipated the long-term needs of His creation. Then He hung the sun and the moon in the sky to rule over the ongoing, ever-changing cycles and seasons of time that would follow.

Let There Be Divine Likeness

In perseverance, godliness—Through perseverance of faith, we learn to walk and think in new ways. Godliness is a fresh and flexible quality of life that honors and reflects the One who made us for Himself. The forming of such character and depth of personality parallels God's purpose in creation. His whole creative process moved toward the moment when He breathed His own likeness into a lump of clay.

Let There Be Community

In godliness, brotherly kindness—Brotherly kindness is the mutual affection of family love. It tracks back to the day our Creator said that it was not good for man to be alone. His intent has not changed. Although our personal relationship to Him is foundational to life, He knows that our thinking and hearts are not complete apart from relationship with others. From the beginning of time, our Father has wanted those who reflect His likeness to have the benefit of like-minded relationships.

Let There Be Love

In brotherly kindness, love—This love is the ultimate in creative thinking. It involves a willingness to esteem others in a way that goes beyond the mutual affections of family love. It is rooted in the teaching and example of Jesus and, even before that, in the opening pages of Genesis. When our first parents turned their backs on their Creator, He did not return the insult. In the days that followed, He showed His willingness to seek the well-being even of those who had no regard for Him.

So what do you think? Are the connections real or imagined? Regardless of your answer, can we pray together:

Father in heaven, we are so inclined to use the darkness in and around us as an excuse to live business as usual. Please do in us, again and again, what You once did with a dark, water-covered earth.

July 2006

HEAVEN

I'M LOOKING FORWARD TO LONG walks with good friends, shared meals without rushing, and endless laughter at no one's expense.

I'm anticipating meaningful work with plenty of time for reading, photography, fishing, and community service. For occasional entertainment, I haven't written off stadiums and ballparks. If my hunch is right, competition between friends will be healthy in heaven. I'm wondering if there might even be hockey without fights, soccer without brawls, and basketball playoffs where losing *well* is valued as much as winning. There may even be a safe form of boxing and NASCAR.

Frivolous speculation? Maybe. Insulting to God? I hope not. I'm trying to imagine a heaven that builds on the good we know while leaving behind the evil.

As a child, I feared heaven would be boring. I missed the point of gold streets and pearly gates. As a ten-year-old, what I really liked doing most was playing baseball, collecting fossils, and hunting frogs.

In the years that followed, the deaths of family members and friends have changed the way I think about heaven. But I still have questions. What will we do after enjoying long embraces, tears of laughter, and catching up? My mind still locks up like an overloaded computer when I try to weigh imponderable questions about a hereafter that will last forever.

Ironically, what gives me the most peace of mind is not cutting loose my imagination, but rather learning to trust. I find rest in the thought that God doesn't want us to know what He has planned for us. I wouldn't be surprised to hear such a God say something like, "If I told you, I'd have to take you." Or, based on the apostle Paul's experience, "If I told you how good it's going to be, I'd have to make life more difficult for you now."

Paul seemed to imply as much when describing what he thought might have been an out-of-body experience. By his own admission, he wasn't sure what happened. But he said he was caught up to paradise where he heard things he wasn't allowed to talk about (2 Corinthians 12:1–4). Apparently, whatever Paul heard was so exhilarating that it would have distracted him from an ongoing dependence upon the grace of God. So, for the duration of Paul's time on earth, the Lord of heaven let him suffer at the hand of Satan to keep him on his knees (2 Corinthians 12:7–9).

I'm convinced that the God who taught Paul to depend on Him one day at a time is now teaching us to rely on Him for an eternity that is beyond our ability to understand.

So how much *does* He want us to know?

Heaven in the Jewish Scriptures

Moses and the prophets tell us only a little about heaven. Asaph, the worship leader of Israel, tells us as much as anyone when he says to his God, "You will guide me with Your counsel, and afterward receive me to glory. Whom have I in heaven but You? And there is none upon earth that I desire besides You" (Psalm 73:24–25).

Later the prophet Isaiah predicts a new relationship between heaven and earth. He foresees a day of international peace, when God will live among His people on earth, when even wild animals will no longer prey on one another (Isaiah 2:4; 65:25). Isaiah envisions the eventual renewal and restoration of earth and sky when he quotes God as saying, "For, behold, I create new heavens and a new earth; and the former shall not be remembered, or come to mind. . . . The voice of weeping shall no longer be heard in her, nor the voice of crying" (Isaiah 65:17–19).

Heaven in the Teachings of Jesus

Jesus spoke often of the kingdom of heaven. It was His way of speaking of the realm of God's rule. In prayer, He taught His disciples to say, "Your kingdom come, Your will be done, on earth as it is in heaven" (Matthew 6:10).

Our Teacher, however, described heaven as more than the seat of divine government. He also called it His Father's house. He told His disciples He was going there to prepare a place for them. "That where I am, there you may be also" (John 14:3). This will be a place of happiness and everlasting reward where treasures don't rust, wear out, or get stolen (Matthew 6:19–20).

Heaven in Revelation

The last book in the Bible brings together into one great vision many themes of God's original creation. In Revelation, heaven comes to earth. The city of God descends to us. God lives among His people and wipes away every "tear from their eyes; there shall be no more death, nor sorrow, nor crying. There shall be no more pain, for the former things have passed away" (Revelation 21:1–4).

Now and Forever

So do I still warm to the possibilities I mentioned earlier? Only in a limited sense. Competition where everyone wins might be the equivalent of gold streets or pearly gates. I don't know. I want to hold those lightly. What I'm more sure about is that our God wants us to hold tightly the anticipation of living with Him forever.

I'm convinced that God is planning one surprise after another, and that heaven will be far more than we ever imagined, not less. And whatever it involves will center on the One who assured His friends with the words, "Let not your heart be troubled . . . . I go to prepare a place for you. And if I go and prepare a place for you, I will come again and receive you to Myself; that where I am, there you may be also" (John 14:1–3).

Father in heaven, we become confused in the darkness of what we don't yet understand. Thank You for being so patient with us. Help us to see that the grace You have shown us today is only a taste of Your ability to use all eternity to surprise us again and again with Your goodness.

December 2005

THE GALAXY

SCIENTISTS TELL US THAT our galaxy is home not only to our own sun and its family of planets, but to billions of other stars. They tell us that our disk-shaped galaxy is about one hundred thousand light-years wide and about two thousand light-years thick. Yet, astronomers tell us that this "cosmic disk" (itself made up of billions of stars) is only one of billions of galaxies known to exist in the universe.

It seems that thinking about such a creation should cause me to praise its Creator. But I have other emotions. I find little comfort in a God whose creation can be measured only in light-years and in billions of galaxies, each made up of billions of stars.

Don't get me wrong. I know that if God were not greater than that which He has created we might all succumb to a creation that is out of control. But what some see through a telescope doesn't awaken my heart in praise until I also think about what others have seen through a microscope. Through a microscope we see the infinite attention to detail that the God of the universe has given to the "little things of life."

The inexpressible systems and details of microscopic life allow me to find great comfort and credibility in the One who reassures us that the hairs of our head are all numbered (Matthew 10:29–31), that a sparrow doesn't fall to the ground unnoticed, and that we are of much more value to Him than many sparrows.

Yet, once again, as I think about the God of little things, the praise slips back into my throat. In His attention to detail, there is danger. Jesus said that we will have to give account for every careless word we have spoken (Matthew 12:36). King David said God not only knows when we stand up and when we sit down, but also what we are thinking (Psalm 139). Solomon said that on a final day of judgment God will examine the secret motives of our heart (Ecclesiastes 12:13–14).

Once again my heart grows cold—until I think of the cross. It is at the cross that my heart finally seems to find wholehearted praise. At Calvary, I can think about the greatness of the God of the galaxies, the One who counts the hairs of my head and the steps of my feet. At Calvary, I can remember the price that it took for Him to pay for the least and worst of my sins, to buy my salvation, and to call me into His undeserved kindness. At Calvary, the God who formed the galaxies becomes the God who loves me—as much as I need to be loved. And for that I want to praise Him. Now, and forever . . .

August 1993

Nations and Politics

ISRAEL

IN THE LAST DAYS, ALL nations of the earth will turn against one small state. As this present age comes to a close, the Bible says the whole world will be united by their shared hatred of the nation of Israel.

What are the implications for ourselves? Are we obliged to take sides with Israel now? Are we bound by our faith to line up with the political struggles of the Jewish people, not only because God will rescue their homeland in the end but because God told Abraham, "I will bless those who bless you, and I will curse him who curses you"? (Genesis 12:3).

The answer is not what we might think. People of the Bible cannot afford to be caught cursing anyone. We have no reason to choose sides against any people—Jewish, Arab, or otherwise. We are called to be peacemakers, lovers of all, and messengers of a gospel that is blind to national and ethnic distinctions. Our calling is to bless people of all nations by our prayers, concerns, and compassion.

Does this mean we are to have no opinion when Palestinians call for the destruction of the State of Israel? Do we ignore the plight of Arab families whose sons die under the fire of Israeli artillery? No. In all matters we are to be motivated by issues of justice and compassion. Even as we pray for the peace of Jerusalem, we have reason to pray for the peace of Damascus, the peace of Cairo, and the peace of Baghdad.

To the extent that we are people of the light, we will be impartial in our love for all people, while knowing that there is no other nation on earth like the nation of Israel. While being one of the smallest countries in the world, she is one huge national museum of theology. Her antiquities are stage and props in an unfolding drama of ethics, philosophy, and history. Her land is a battlefield for the war of the gods.

Her people are known not only as a chosen people but as survivors of the Holocaust. Her wild animals are morality lessons, while her agriculture and greening desert landscapes look like a fulfillment of prophetic visions.

No other nation on earth has been destroyed, scattered to the four corners of the globe, and then regathered as the focus of world attention. No other nation has been chosen by God to be so shamed for her sins before a watching world. No other nation has been lifted so high or dragged so low.

Israel is the land of the Bible, a book that was produced by Jewish prophets yet repeatedly criticizes the Jewish people for failing to be the servant nation she was chosen to be.

Israel is the land of Jesus, who lived like no other man has ever lived but was rejected by the very people to whom He appeared as Messiah. Israel is a land of faith, which gave birth to the three great monotheistic religions of the world but remains host to one of the most secular and atheistic people on earth.

Israel is a land of contrasts. Small in size but immeasurable in significance. Eternally chosen by God, but temporarily rejected by Him before all the nations of the earth. Her religious capital has a name that means "City of Peace," yet it has been one of the most continuous sources of conflict the world has ever known. Jerusalem, built on the mountains of Israel, separated by only a few miles from the valley city of Jericho, is one of the oldest and lowest spots on earth.

Israel, land of two great bodies of water. One, a great natural reservoir known as the Galilee, receives water from the melting snow of Mount Hermon and waters the whole region. The other, eighty miles to the south, collects all water that comes to it, has no outlets, and is known as the Dead Sea. Ironically, however, even in its deadness, this salt sea produces, through modern mining technology, enough phosphates to fertilize the farmlands not only of Israel but of the world.

No other nation tells us more about God, more about ourselves, or more about one another. No other nation declares by its reemergence in time that there is a God who deserves to be feared and loved and obeyed. No other nation exists as a declaration to the world that in the records of her history we find our roots and in the predictions of her prophets we find our future.

Those who have the opportunity to visit this land are not necessarily made better by walking where Jesus walked. Hearts are not changed by touching the Wailing Wall, or by gazing into the Armageddon landscape of the Jezreel Valley. But those who visit this land, read its history, or look at pictures of its mountains and valleys have before them a tangible evidence of the greatest story ever told, something more provocative and compelling than breaking network news.

In a world of multicultural pluralism we find in Israel the story of a Creator who refuses to give His glory to the idols of human likeness. Here we find real places that were inhabited by real people who in their time became witnesses to a God who revealed Himself to one nation for the sake of all. Here we find the homes, the battlefields, and the graves of a people who have given the world a boundless treasure of history and philosophy and faith. Here in the stones and rocks of Israel we find the sheep and goats, the mountains and valleys, Zions and Gehennas of our own lives. Here we touch with our hands relics of a story that people of all nations can accept and embrace to their own eternal salvation.

Here is a land chosen by God to tell all the world that He alone deserves to be worshiped, that He alone is the One we sin against, that He alone has offered a Sacrifice adequate to pay for the worst of our sins, that He alone is willing to forgive as a gift, in exchange for the simple offer of our own surrender and trust.

November 1998

THE ARAB-ISRAELI CONFLICT

BAD BLOOD IN THE MIDEAST flows from generation to generation like an ancient river of oil and water. From the days of Abram to our own breaking news, there seems to be no end to the fatal rivalry of Ishmael and Isaac.

The conflict that began with patriarchs of the Arab and Jewish people affects all of us. It costs us at the gas pump. It divides us at church. Some of us think our faith leads us to be pro-Israel. Some think a good Samaritan theology favors the Palestinians.

An Inclination to Side with Israel

My pattern has been to side with those who are sympathetic to the Jewish struggle for a homeland because . . .

1. we remember that the God of the Bible gave the "promised land" to Israel.
2. we are embarrassed by the anti-Semitism of our church fathers and want to disassociate ourselves from any hint of the hatred seen in Haman or Hitler.

3. we believe the events of the Holocaust show the Jewish people's need for a homeland.
4. we see in Israel's rebirth not only evidence for the God of the Bible but for our view of prophecy as well.
5. most important, we hear God saying to Abram, "I will bless those who bless you, and I will curse him who curses you; and in you all the families of the earth shall be blessed" (Genesis 12:3).

A Tendency to Forget Arab Interests

It's easy to forget that . . .

1. as people of the gospel we are to bless all and to curse no one (Romans 12:14); and
2. while supporting Israel's need for a homeland, we need to remember the non-Jewish families whose ancestors have lived in the Holy Land for centuries.

Don't get me wrong. I don't want to betray the trust of our Jewish friends. I just deeply regret that I have heard the cries of Sarah and Isaac while being blind to the tears of Hagar and Ishmael. I haven't done well in distinguishing between what God is doing in Israel and what Israel herself is doing without God.

The Unequal Legacy of Ishmael

From the beginning, Ishmael seemed to be the son of a bad idea. Although he was born into the home of Abram and Sarah, Ishmael was conceived as a result of his father's relationship with an Egyptian woman named Hagar.

At Sarah's suggestion, Abram had a child by her live-in housekeeper. But the solution itself gave birth to trouble. Later, when Sarah miraculously conceived a son of her own, the stage was set for conflict between the two boys and their mothers. At Sarah's urging, Abram put Hagar and Ishmael out of the house.

According to Genesis 21:17–20, heaven responded tenderly to the tears of Hagar. The angel of the Lord gave her son a name which means "God will hear" (Genesis 16:11). God Himself was with Ishmael (Genesis 21:20) and promised to make him into a great nation (Genesis 17:20).

In the process of befriending Hagar and Ishmael, however, God seems to warn of the painful consequences that will result from Abram's actions. Of the child he and his wife threw into the wilderness, God said, "He shall be a wild man [literally wild donkey]. His hand shall be against every man, and every man's hand against him. And he shall dwell in the presence of all his brethren" (Genesis 16:12). Ishmael seemed destined to show us that hurt people hurt people. Being thrown out of the house probably contributed not only to his own approach to life but to a survival attitude that became a part of his legacy.

The Need for Balance and Fairness

Several factors can help to balance our understanding of what God was doing with Isaac and Ishmael:

1. God's choice of Abraham, Isaac, and Jacob as the "line of promise" was intended to be for the good of everyone, not just their own children. From the beginning God made it clear that He was choosing one nation for the sake of all (Genesis 12:1–3).
2. Although Ishmael was predicted to be a "wild donkey," there were equally unflattering names and predictions in the Jewish legacy. Jacob, father of the twelve tribes of

Israel, was given a birth name that meant "betrayer, or deceiver." Later the prophets of Israel described their own nation as a "lusty donkey," as a "prostitute" (Jeremiah 2), and as a community that made Sodom and Gomorrah look good by comparison (Ezekiel 16:48–52).

3. The legacy of the chosen people was a heavy burden. They were chosen not only to show the whole world the power and goodness of the one true God, but also to show all the nations of the earth what happens when people ignore and wander from the love and wisdom of their Creator (Deuteronomy 28–30).

4. Even if God's hand can be seen in Israel's presence in the land, we need to remember her spiritual condition. Israel today mirrors what the prophet Ezekiel foresaw in his vision of the dry bones. Hundreds of years before Christ, God predicted that in the last days Israel would come together physically before being reborn spiritually (Ezekiel 37:1–4).

5. Israel's efforts to secure her borders are like Abram's and Sarah's attempts to have a son by Hagar. History is repeating itself. Human solutions once again are multiplying into human problems and pain.

And how are we to respond? We can respond with awe, because what God has chosen to do and to allow is unfolding before our eyes. We can respond with discernment, because there is a difference between what God is doing in Israel and what Israel herself is doing without God. And we can respond with goodwill, because the God who has promised to take care of us has asked us in turn to bless all and to curse no one (Romans 12:14).

Father in heaven, I have been so slow to see that my love tends not only to be self-serving but full of prejudice as well. Help me not only to hear the cries of Sarah and Isaac but to see the tears of Hagar and Ishmael. Please help us to see that the conflict between Arabs and Israelis is a picture of how much we all need the grace and peace that can be found only in You.

May 2002

WHY ISRAEL CAN'T BE IGNORED

WHETHER LOVED OR HATED, Israel is a magnet. Although no larger than the state of New Jersey, she draws journalists, statesmen, and tourists from all over the world to a few acres of the most contested real estate on earth.

Arriving from many nations, Jewish, Christian, and Muslim pilgrims stream through Ben Gurion airport in Tel Aviv to see with their own eyes the cities, mountains, and valleys that are home to some of their deepest thoughts and hopes.

The People of This Land

Most of those who come to Israel discover a common bond with the people of the land. Almost everyone they find here traces their ancestry back to the same father. Although the region was occupied before and after by people of other family groups, almost everyone claims to be related through a man named Abraham. Ironically Abraham, whose name means "father of many," was childless until the age of eighty-five.

Arab people see themselves as the children of Abraham's first son, Ishmael. Jewish people trace their lineage through a second son, Isaac. And Christians see themselves as the spiritual children of Abraham (Galatians 3:7).

From within this family tree, however, God chose the line of Isaac to be the "branch" through which He would reveal Himself to the world. In time, it became apparent that this branch would bear not only the fruit of God's blessing but the burden of heaven's correction as well.

The Story of This Land

The unfolding drama of "the chosen people" is more than the greatest story ever told. It is also the longest running show in history. For the last four thousand years the curtains of time have risen and fallen on a land that has been like a great stage positioned on a land bridge and the trade routes between Africa, Asia, and Europe.

With timeless significance the people of this land have told the story of a great King who let His own Son die in order to save the lives and future of His people.

The times and people of this story have made the land into an enormous national museum of history. Here thoughtful visitors climb steps and walk corridors carpeted with the hopes and dreams of a nation. The irony is that this national museum is not designed to showcase the treasures of a royal dynasty. Instead, its halls and steps wind their way to a main exhibit built in honor of a lowly rabbi-carpenter from Nazareth.

The Messiah of This Land

There has never been another man like Him. Known in His day as a rabbi from the wrong side of town, His miraculous life, profound wisdom, premature death, and astounding resurrection have given Him a status greater than Abraham. Calendars of the world count from the year of His birth.

Jewish prophets anticipated His coming. They spoke of a King who would bring peace to the world (Isaiah 2:1–4). They foresaw that this "Anointed One" would be conceived within the womb of a virgin (Isaiah 7:14). He would be called "Mighty God" (Isaiah 9:6). He would be born in Bethlehem, the city of David (Micah 5:2). They also predicted that this Servant of God would die as a lamb led to the slaughter—to bear the wrongs of others (Isaiah 53; Daniel 9:26; Zechariah 12:10).

The Witnesses of This Land

In the region of Galilee's great freshwater lake, the Jewish and Gentile people from shoreline communities met this teacher face to face. Together they saw Him heal crippled bodies. Some saw Him walk on water. They saw Him feed thousands of people with four loaves of bread and a couple of fish.

The Messiah they saw has left His impact on every generation since. His answer to our spiritual needs is what led Blaise Pascal, a seventeenth-century physicist, mathematician, and Christian philosopher, to say, "There is a God-shaped vacuum in the heart of every man which cannot be filled by any created thing, but only by God the Creator, made known through Jesus Christ."

The Real Importance of This Land

The real importance of this land is that it bore the footprints of our God as He walked among us. It bore the weight of the best man who ever lived as He hung on an executioner's cross. It gave us witnesses who reported His resurrection from the dead three days later. Then the cumulative evidence of this land asks us, "What are you going to do with Him?"

Each of us needs to answer this question. The witnesses of this land invite us to come closer. The gospel writer Luke brings us close enough to overhear a conversation that occurred as the long-awaited Messiah hung dying between two criminals being executed at His side. While one of these men mocked Jesus because He was dying as they were, the other was more thoughtful and introspective. The second criminal said to the first, "We receive the due reward of our deeds; but this Man has done nothing wrong." Then he turned to Jesus and said, "Remember me when You come into Your Kingdom." Jesus said, "Today you will be with Me in Paradise" (Luke 23:43). By a simple act of trust, a condemned, dying criminal received heaven's pardon and everlasting life.

All of the chapters of Israel's history point to the death and resurrection of the One who made that promise to a dying man. As the Messiah of Israel was dying, He used a condemned criminal to show all of us how we too can be with Him forever. His words were for all of us. He will bring to His eternal home all who say from their hearts, "I've done wrong. I believe You died for my sins. I accept You as my Savior and entrust myself to You."

Those who make this decision understand why Israel cannot be ignored. It's no wonder that, whether loved or hated, Israel is a magnet. This land is the stage for the greatest story ever told. It is a national museum of history and theology. It is one great archaeological dig for the land of the Bible. This is the battlefield for our souls, our hearts, and our minds.

July 2002

THE HOLOCAUST

HAVING JUST RETURNED FROM a work assignment in Israel, I've been reminded again of the Jewish commitment to *never forget* their national Holocaust.

I've also come back with a renewed concern for friends who see a link between anti-Semitism and the New Testament. While recalling discussions with one of those friends, I'm writing:

Dear Eli,
Hope you're doing well. Sure enjoyed our conversations during my recent stay in Jerusalem.

Since you are aware of my confidence in the Gospel accounts, I appreciate your willingness to talk so freely about your own spiritual journey. I've thought a lot about your struggle to believe in a God who would allow the Holocaust.

I also keep thinking about how different our backgrounds have been. You grew up in a home where your mother, after being the only sister in her family to survive the death camps, could not talk about God. I was raised in a home where we were taught to see our Creator not only in nature and in the daily provisions of life, but also in the history of your people.

I've also thought a lot about your observation that some people came out of the Holocaust with a complete loss of faith, while others responded not only with belief but also with deep devotion to God.

Your candor was refreshing. And when you asked if I thought you were being unreasonable, I knew I could quickly say, "no"—while sensing that you had asked a very difficult question.

Part of me wants to say that the systematic, state-sponsored killing of your people had everything to do with human evil and nothing to do with God. But then I'm reminded of the God of the Jewish Scriptures who had His reasons for allowing pagan nations to tear down the walls of Jerusalem, while breaking His own heart in the process.

I've also thought about your comment that the closest you come to sensing God is in the wilderness. I too have felt the wonder of wide-open space and silence. Away from the sounds of the city, I've sensed not only the presence of God but also the capacity for moral choice and consequence that eventually bring me back to the commotion of the city.

On a couple of occasions I've heard the air-raid sirens that wail in Israel on your Holocaust Remembrance Day. I've watched as you stopped whatever you were doing and stood in silence for one minute. In that annual moment of remembrance, I think I've seen something of what it means to be a "chosen people." From the days of Abraham, your people have been center stage in the story of human civilization. Sometimes you have been a guiding light for your neighbors. On other occasions, your story has been like an unnerving siren reminding us that something terrible has happened to our world.

No, your ancestors didn't ask to be a "chosen people." Nor do I believe the outcome would have been any different if God had formed or miraculously preserved any other ethnic group. Because human nature is universal, the story would have been the same, under a different name. It could just as well have been the French, the Germans, or the Japanese who had to face the reality that it's hard to be a "chosen people." Any other nation chosen to be the people of Messiah would bear the same burden.

In mentioning Messiah, I recognize your suspicion that anti-Semitism has roots in Gospel records that portray your people as "Christ-killers." Even though the New Testament is written by Jewish authors about a Jewish Messiah, non-Jewish people have made far too much of the fact that some Jewish leaders called for Jesus' death. What too many have forgotten is that the rabbi from Nazareth died voluntarily, under the authority of a Roman governor, and at the hands of brutal Roman executioners. When Jewish people are singularly blamed for the death of Jesus, the good news of God's own sacrifice for the atonement of our sin is missed. Those who point the finger at Jewish people also misrepresent the spirit of the New Testament that shows God's love for Israel (Matthew 23:37; Romans 9:1–5; 10:1–4).

But Eli, if you are not ready to read the New Testament, I wish you would at least read again the ancient story of Job. The sages of Israel have long treasured his life as evidence that people do not suffer in proportion to their sins. Instead, as the Hebrew Scriptures show, God sometimes calls people like Job, the Israelites, and His Messiah to suffer for the sake of others. Job was a good man who suffered to show the rest of us that Satan—not God—is the source of evil. Israel's troubles help us to see the danger of walking away from the protection of God.

And the sufferings of God's sinless Messiah are for the atonement of all who have left God to go their own way (Isaiah 53).

I don't believe the Hebrew Scriptures give us any reason to see the tragic events of the Holocaust as a picture of God's individual judgment on those who died. Eternity alone will show what heaven was seeing in the hearts of those who suffered in such abandonment and darkness. But if this event had any relationship to the other tragic national days described in the Hebrew Scriptures, then a chosen nation's troubles can be a spiritual wake-up call for all who are watching.

If I know anything about the God and Messiah of Israel, His heart was broken by the suffering of Jewish people in death camps of inexpressible evil. Yet, with irony that goes beyond words, the tears and the agony of those dark days are part of the wisdom God used in giving us the freedom to choose our own path. And if, in choosing our own way, we miss the rescue of God's Messiah, it is far more loving for Him to sound a siren than to be silent.

Eli, I hope this will help you to better understand where I'm coming from. I hope to hear from you when you get a chance.

Sincerely,
Mart

SHOULD WE FORGIVE TERRORISTS?

THE FRONT PAGE OF OUR local newspaper carried the story of peace activists protesting the use of bombs to fight international terrorism. The article included a photo of a child carrying a sign asking, "What Would Jesus Do?"

The question on the sign is important. Jesus said that if we don't forgive others, the Father in heaven will not forgive us (Matthew 6:14–15). But was He telling us to forgive those who have not had a change of heart? Not according to the rest of the Scriptures.

Don't misunderstand me. I'm not an advocate of vengeance. I need forgiveness as much as anyone. I see how unbecoming it is to receive mountains of forgiveness from heaven, only to withhold handfuls from those who hurt us on earth. But if we are not careful with forgiveness, we may unintentionally strengthen the grip of dangerous people.

Let's take another look at what the Bible asks of us . . .

1. There is a difference between love and forgiveness. God loves everyone, and He shows mercy to all (Matthew 5:45). But He does not forgive everyone. He offers forgiveness with conditions because there are some attitudes He will not forgive. As compassionate as He is, He won't lift the burden of guilt from those who refuse to acknowledge their need for mercy.

But someone says, "You're missing the point. Vengeance is God's business, not ours. We don't forgive to let those who have harmed us off the hook. We forgive to turn the offenders over to God and to get the bitterness and anger out of our own stomachs. If we don't forgive, our own anger will consume us."

Vengeance does belong to God alone. But will a watching world see us acting nobly and lovingly when we offer forgiveness to unrepentant, dangerous people? My guess is that others will think we are dangerously naive and only forgiving for our own emotional survival.

2. Everyone can be forgiven, but only some qualify. God forgives repentant people. His heart reaches out to those who are contrite and broken (Isaiah 66:2). But He does not forgive those who consciously hide and cling to their wrongs. Neither does He teach us to automatically forgive everyone who has wronged us.

Instead, the God of the Bible teaches us to pray for our enemies. He teaches us to lovingly confront those who have harmed us and to forgive those who acknowledge their wrong (Matthew 18:15–18; Luke 17:1–4; 1 Corinthians 5:1–8; 2 Corinthians 2:6–11).

3. Christ's warnings need to be understood. We can't afford to misunderstand the words of Jesus: "If you do not forgive men their trespasses, neither will your Father forgive your trespasses" (Matthew 6:15). He wasn't teaching us to automatically forgive everyone who harms us. His warning was for those whose hearts are hard and unrelenting toward those who ask for our forgiveness. His loving anger is a warning of what happens when we refuse to give repentant people the mercy we ourselves have received (Matthew 18:23–35).

4. Neither love nor forgiveness eliminates the need for social justice and national security. Acts of terrorism are not just crimes against individuals. By design they are attacks against the state. As a result they fall into a different category than personal insult and harm. Assaults on national security are similar to the threats we find King David responding to in some of his national songs of judgment.

In several of his well-known Old Testament psalms, David called for the utter destruction of the enemy. Because he expressed a cry for judgment rather than mercy, many think that his prayers are inconsistent with the spirit of Christ. But it's important to realize that when David wrote as the king of Israel, his cries for help were not only for himself but for the security of his people (Psalms 5, 11, 17, 35, 55, 59, 69, 109, 137, and 140).

Much of the Bible shows that there is a time for war, just as there is a time for peace. Although war has terrible consequences, leaders who love their people must take severe action against aggressors. The apostle Paul supported this governmental justice when he wrote that the authorities do not bear the sword in vain but are God's servants to execute justice on those who do evil (Romans 13:4).

5. To love is more important than to forgive. To care, even for those we must go to war against, is Christlike. Even when our military is dropping bombs on those our leaders have declared enemies of the state, love teaches us to cry inside for those who are suffering. Many, after all, are suffering not for their own wrongs, but for the wrongs of their leaders.

When a terrorist is killed, we can be thankful that the person no longer poses a threat to others. But God takes no pleasure in the death of His enemies (Ezekiel 33:11), and neither will we if our hearts are filled with the compassion of Christ.

6. Love fulfills the principle of forgiveness. As followers of Christ, we are to be known for our forgiveness. Even more, we are to be known for our love (Galatians 5:14). All biblical principles can be misapplied and misused if they are not motivated by a heart of enlightened love.

But what does this love look like? It is a love that walks in the clothes of the wisdom and principles of the Bible. This love is what prompted the apostle Paul to write, "For all the law is fulfilled in one word, even in this: 'You shall love your neighbor as yourself'" (Galatians 5:14).

Christlike love needs to set the tone and rhythm of our lives. We are to be known not only for our willingness to offer timely forgiveness but also for our willingness to stand against oppressors, while acting courageously in behalf of those who have no voice or strength of their own.

Father in heaven, sometimes we have forgiven only for our own sake, rather than for Your sake and the good of others. Please teach us to forgive as You have forgiven us. Show us how to compassionately stand with victims. Help us confront and stop oppressors, without taking delight in their pain or death.

March 2002

ETHNIC MIXING

EVEN THOUGH RACIALLY mixed marriages are becoming more common, some still resent it when a member of their own ethnic community marries an outsider. Others are convinced that such marriages are morally or spiritually wrong. Until concluding that mixed marriages do have spiritual implications, I wasn't sure I wanted to think through the subject in the presence of those who might be hurt or offended by my attempts to find a biblical perspective.

Do the Scriptures give us reason to believe that Asian, African, and European bloodlines should be kept pure? What about lesser ethnic distinctions? Some families believe Dutch stock should not be mixed with Swedish or German gene pools (as in my own parents' case when they married, with some resentment from Holland-born relatives).

To test our thinking, let's give a hearing to those who believe ethnic differences are a part of the divine order. Such a person might say, "Racial purity is a righteous idea. Whether we like it or not, our Creator made the races different. The same God who made all living creatures to reproduce after their own kind is the One who made Asians, Africans, Europeans, and Latinos. How could it be right for us to blend distinctions He conceived? Furthermore," such a person might argue, "according to the book of Genesis all bloodlines are not equal. Through Noah, God predestined the descendants of Ham, who migrated to Africa, to be a servant race. We may not like all of this. We may think we are sophisticated enough to override God's purposes. But according to the Bible, our Creator is the source of our differences, and it's dangerous to think we know better than Him."

Some might see such an argument for ethnic purity as an example of conservative, Bible-believing conviction. Let me suggest, however, why I think using the Scriptures to condemn racially mixed marriages is an example of theological and biblical confusion. Let's see if the Scriptures can give us help in evaluating the validity of Afro-European marriages.

1. We were alike before we were different. The Scriptures repeatedly show that all of us have roots from the same parents (Acts 17:26). Before there were differences of skin tone, facial features, and language, we were alike. First, we were the sons and daughters of Adam and Eve. After a terrible flood wiped out everyone except one family, the gene pool was narrowed back down to Noah's family. For this reason there's no merit to the idea that God expects people to protect racial purity by reproducing after their own kind. All families of the earth share equally, not only in the gene pool of humanity but in the image and likeness of God. We may be inclined to belittle one another by failing to identify with the thoughts and emotions of people who look or sound different than we do. But the Bible clearly says that we all have the same human blood running through our veins.

2. God did not predestine Africans to be a servant race. The idea that Africans were predestined to be a servant class comes from a misreading of a biblical story. It relates to a curse pronounced by Noah after learning that his son Ham had told his brothers he'd seen their father lying naked in a drunken stupor (Genesis 9:20–27). From Noah's reaction to Ham, we conclude he felt that Ham had shown him disrespect. A closer look shows that Noah did not curse all of Ham's descendants, many of whom migrated south into Africa. The curse settled specifically on Canaan, the fourth son of Ham, whose descendants eventually moved into the area now occupied by the nation of Israel. Noah's curse fell on the Canaanites, who were judged for their idolatrous, sexual excesses.

3. Moses married an Ethiopian woman. When Aaron and Miriam, Moses' brother and sister, spoke against Moses "because of his Ethiopian wife," God showed His displeasure with their criticism, but did not indicate He had a problem with Moses' mixed marriage. God showed disapproval of Miriam's condemnation of Moses by striking Miriam's skin with leprosy for seven days (Numbers 12:1–15). I doubt it's a coincidence that God turned Miriam's skin "leper white" in judgment.

4. Hearts are more important to God than skin color. While the New Testament urges followers of Christ not to enter into a binding relationship with someone who does not believe in Christ (2 Corinthians 6:14), it never says anything about avoiding people with a different shade of skin. Never does the New Testament give us reason to believe that God wants us to stay within our own ethnic profile. But a concerned black or white parent may ask, "What about the social burden carried by partners in a racially mixed relationship? Isn't marriage difficult enough without facing enormous cultural differences too?" These are important questions. Ethnic and temperamental differences that are appealing in courtship sometimes become the very differences that are most difficult to tolerate as the marriage matures. But however difficult our differences, we must remember that God is more concerned about the attitudes of our hearts than about skin color.

The real issue isn't what we think about racially mixed marriages. It's how deeply we care about all who've been created by Christ—and for whom He died.

August 1999

ABUSE OF AUTHORITY

THERE IS A FINE LINE between the healthy and unhealthy use of power. At any time, even the best of leaders can begin making decisions that increasingly put their own interests before the needs of others.

The misuse of authority, however, is not always subtle. History tells the stories of countless leaders who boldly acted as if their position placed them above real accountability.

Biblical Examples of Misused Power

In Bible times, the sons of Samuel used their appointments as judges of Israel to take bribes, pervert justice, and accumulate personal wealth. Later, God's choice for the first king of Israel, Saul, abused his power in an effort to kill the man chosen to be his successor. When David became king, he misused the authority of the throne of Israel to commit adultery with the wife of one of his officers. Then David conspired to have Bathsheba's husband killed.

Centuries later, a little-known church leader named Diotrephes misused his position by denouncing others to elevate himself. He was so protective of his own position that he would not even welcome the apostle John into his congregation (3 John 1:9–10). We don't know how Diotrephes publicly explained his lack of hospitality. But privately he might have assumed that all he had done for the church entitled him to unchallenged prominence in the group.

The Patterns of Abuse

Whether it is in ancient times or today, abuse of authority always involves a harmful and destructive pattern of leadership that diverts organizational power for personal use at the expense of others.

A culture of fear

Such abuse of authority thrives in a culture where people fear one another. Leaders are afraid of losing power. Subordinates know the danger of confronting those in authority. Loyalty is emphasized to distract from what is really happening. Mutual intimidation lies just under the surface of what seems safe to talk about or question.

A culture of confusion

In church or para-church groups, leaders sometimes use spiritual language that implies they have a private line to God. The result is that the group learns to hear the teaching or prayerful decisions of leadership as if they were listening to God. Such confusion leads to trouble.

A culture of control and exclusion

When spiritual overseers are not held accountable to fair process and well-defined checks and balances, they can impose their will in ways that go beyond their rightful sphere of control. Such leaders may remove a noncompliant person from the group, not for the sake of the organization but as a means to protect their own leadership. By threatening exclusion for noncompliance, leaders can require submission in matters that are more personal than public, more cultural than biblical, and more arbitrary than fairly reasoned. Ironically, abusive leaders often suggest that their own accountability to God places them above criticism and question, without granting the same freedom to others.

In the noise and commotion of such abuse, phrases like "touch not the Lord's anointed" or "obey those that have the rule over you" are used, not to promote a healthy fear of the Lord but rather an unhealthy fear of men.

A Better Example

Jesus' example of leadership is a corrective to such abuse of authority. In His kingdom, leaders think and act like servants. They hear the questions and cries of those who are hurting. They give others the consideration they want for themselves.

In Jesus' kingdom, elders and deacons do not correct someone else without first working on their own faults (Luke 6:39, 41–42). They remember the Lord's words: "A disciple is not above his teacher, but everyone who is perfectly trained will be like his teacher" (Luke 6:40).

One Leader's Inspired Counsel

Listen to what one of Jesus' understudies tells us. Watch for the value the apostle Peter puts on heartfelt service. Note that he wants both elders and church members to serve God not by coercion but because they desire to. Peter writes to fellow elders: "Shepherd the flock of God which is among you, serving as overseers, *not by compulsion but willingly,* not for dishonest gain but *eagerly; nor as being lords over those entrusted to you, but being examples* to the flock" (1 Peter 5:2–3, emphasis added).

Spiritual shepherds are not to "lord it over" the flock of God. Just as overseers, elders, and deacons are not to be pressed into service, neither are they to intimidate, shame, or compel others to serve, to give, or to follow. Even when confronting false teachers, representatives of Christ are not to be authoritarian in style, but "gentle to all, able to teach, patient, in humility correcting those who are in opposition" (2 Timothy 2:24–25).

Sooner or later, therefore, we need to realize that we don't honor even the most trusted spiritual leaders by believing everything they say. We give them their rightful place when we weigh their words, ask important questions, and dig into the text of their message for ourselves.

The New Testament record of Acts honors the citizens of Berea precisely because they did not passively accept what they were taught by Paul and Silas. Instead, our record of the New Testament church says of the Bereans, "These were more fair-minded than those in Thessalonica, in that they received the word with all readiness, and searched the Scriptures daily to find out whether these things were so" (Acts 17:11).

The implication is clear. God does not give His leaders power and authority to control people, but to speak a truth that sets people free.

Father in heaven, please help us to love and reflect the leadership of Your Son. Teach us to follow Him by listening to the questions and cries of the weakest among us, while reserving strong words only for those who are using their authority at the expense of those they have been called to protect.

Father, may those of us who are in supportive roles learn to respect those who are leading, while also learning to think for ourselves. Please give us hearts that are ready to hear Your Word, eager to learn, and ready to express, by our actions, the truth and grace of Your Son.

April 2006

THE POLITICAL CHALLENGE

IS IT WISE FOR FOLLOWERS of Christ to be involved in the social debate over public policy?

The question of political activism is dividing Christian groups right down the middle. Some are convinced that it is our moral responsibility to use our civil rights to "capture our culture for Christ" and "reclaim our national Christian heritage." They reason that the first amendment ("Congress shall make no law respecting an establishment of religion, or prohibiting the free exercise thereof") is not meant to keep religion out of government as much as to keep government out of religion. Others are just as convinced that the wrong mix of religion and politics can be explosively destructive to all.

Both sides make good points. One group reasons that it is our calling to be "salt and light" in our society. They point to the mistakes of churches that remained silent about slavery, a woman's right to vote, or the civil rights of ethnic minorities. The other side warns, however, that whenever religious movements have been married to governmental authority or political parties, people of faith have traded their spiritual message for a political reputation.

The argument is not just American. As we enter the twenty-first century, people all over the world are talking about the role of religious fundamentalists in government. While Christians in America debate this issue among ourselves, similar discussions are occurring among Jewish, Muslim, and Hindu populations. As societies of the world become increasingly international and pluralistic, minority groups are becoming equally sensitive to any group that tries to use the political process to "lord it over" other religious or ethnic interests.

The Need to Speak Two Languages

As our own culture changes, I believe part of the answer requires followers of Christ to know how and when to speak a second language. We have a biblical responsibility to speak the language of our mission to anyone who is looking for spiritual answers. On the other hand, it is our constitutional responsibility as US citizens to speak the language of liberty and justice for all. While trying to lead others to Christ, we still need to be able to say to a Hindu, or a Buddhist, or a Muslim, "I may not agree with what you are saying, but I will fight for your right to say it. In addition, I will use my social influence to seek just and fair treatment not only for my family but for yours as well."

The Need for Wise Distinctions

Jesus Himself taught us to balance the duties of our dual citizenship. Rather than discounting either civil or spiritual responsibilities, He told His followers to give to Caesar what belongs to Caesar, and to God what belongs to God (Matthew 22:21).

In this light I'd like to suggest some distinctions that I believe are important to consider as we think about our obligations to both God and government. In the following list of comparisons, a "political voice" is one that speaks for its public, and a "prophetic voice" is a messenger who speaks on behalf of God.

❖ A political voice often mobilizes support by concealing its own faults while calling attention to the weaknesses and limitations of the opposition. A prophetic voice is first brought to its knees by its own wrongs and failures (as were Isaiah and Nehemiah).

❖ A political voice tends to speak for the special-interest groups it represents. As a result, it is likely to confront the sins of the right but not the sins of the left—or the sins of the left and not the sins of the right. A prophetic voice, in the best sense, represents the interests of all. The messenger of God, therefore, lovingly and faithfully confronts sins on all bands of the social spectrum. Heaven's representative confronts the sins of the wealthy and the powerful as well as the sins of the poor and the weak.

❖ A political voice calls for external regulation and legislation that often focuses on curbing the freedom of its opponents. A prophetic voice calls on all to submit themselves to God for a personal change of heart, resulting in voluntary self-limitation.

❖ A political voice often represents the special interests of supporters who expect material benefits or social influence in exchange for their donations and votes. A prophetic voice represents the interests of God in a manner that seeks justice and mercy for all members of a society.

❖ A political voice may have to settle for strategies of compromise to maintain an adequate base of support. A faithful prophetic voice does not waver from timeless values and perspectives, and is willing to be "one crying in the wilderness" with accountability to God alone.

❖ A political voice works for change through the strength of opinion polls, ballots, and governmental appointments. A prophetic voice calls for change through loving confrontation and persuasion—relying on whatever voluntary change the Spirit of God and His Word will make in the hearts of hearers.

❖ A political voice rises and falls on the changing tides of public sentiment. A prophetic voice rests on the ultimate and eternal authority of God.

❖ A political voice seeks changes in social behavior by applying the external pressures of law-making and enforcement. A prophetic voice calls for change in individual hearts as the means of transforming a society.

Father in heaven, we need Your wisdom. Please show us how to be good citizens of both heaven and earth. Help us to be heard in behalf of those who need a voice. Teach us to seek justice, to love mercy, and to walk humbly before You. Give us sound judgment in whatever opportunity we have to contribute to good public policy. But please don't let us be known more for our belief in good laws than for our love for Your Son who died for us.

November 2002

TOLERANCE

PLURALISTIC CULTURES LIKE our own put a high value on tolerance. In matters of personal morality and religious faith, most things are tolerable except intolerance itself.

The healthy side of "politically correct" tolerance is that it attempts to assure mutual respect among people of different religious and cultural perspectives. The dangerous side is that children of such cultures are raised to consider all points of view as equally valid.

Where does this leave those of us who do not believe everything is relative or that all religious or philosophical views are equally valid? Should we be angry about a society that tolerates sexual immorality and philosophical relativism, while at the same time becomes increasingly intolerant of the Christian mission? Should we be angry that a nation which used to assume Judeo-Christian values is increasingly resistant to the Christian gospel?

If we are not careful, we might end up on the wrong side of this issue.

It is easy for us to feel insulted and intimidated by a government and society that attempts to marginalize people of "fundamentalist" conviction. It is easy to feel that we must fight all attempts to define us out of a government "of the people, by the people, and for the people." It is easy to assume that because "sin is a reproach to any nation," our mission is to make sure that government is a friend or at least a protector of our mission to evangelize. It is easy to assume that "tolerance of sin" is all wrong.

Policies of tolerance, however, are not all wrong. They form the mutual ground on which we can stand with non-Christians to press the point that while all religious points of view might be tolerated in a free society, all are not equally valid.

While the God of the Bible teaches us not to tolerate pride, greed, or sexual immorality in ourselves or in the lives of those who take the name of Christ, He teaches His people to tolerate sin in the lives of those who do not yet know Christ as Savior (1 Corinthians 5:7–13). To tolerate sin in the lives of non-Christian neighbors does not mean we condone their sin. It means we seek to patiently love them to Christ, as God has loved us to Himself.

As Christians we must not only pray for our enemies and give them reason to come to Christ, but we must also defend their right to disagree with us and reach conclusions inconsistent with our own. While we do not agree with such views or consider them equally valid, we must fight for their right to hold them.

What we must not do is argue our case and vote our morality in public forums for the purpose of "reclaiming our rights" or "to protect our children from the evils of unbelievers." Those who don't yet know Christ need to feel our compassion more than our desire for control. They need to see that we are not motivated by fear for ourselves, but by love for them.

Our path will not be easy. Our mission to tell our world about "one mediator between God and man" will be seen by multi-cultural societies as one more form of religious fundamentalism that is especially dangerous.

Anti-conversion policy will undoubtedly become a mark of the coming global village. The world of the future will offer religious freedom, while at the same time censuring any group that seeks converts.

World governments are under growing pressure to adopt policy designed to protect religious groups from threatening one another. The Republic of Turkey, for instance, offers religious freedom while at the same time taking a tough stance against any religious group that attempts to make converts from outside of its own members. While such laws seem designed to frustrate Christian missions, they were actually drafted to eliminate conflict between competing Muslim sects. The issue is not only the Christian message, but any religious message that threatens to disrupt societal cohesion.

All of this seems threatening. But this is no time to throw up our hands or throw in the towel. We have merely lived long enough to come full circle to first-century conditions. The church was born in a time marked by sexual immorality, and by the tolerance of all kinds of gods. The church was born in a day that tolerated almost anything except a faith that lovingly pointed others to the Lord of lords.

Father, help us to love others in the way You have instructed us (2 Timothy 2:24–26). Help us to live in the spirit of those apostles who found in a hostile environment an opportunity to love their enemies and to obey You rather than man.

July 1997

Personalities and
Relationships

THE VALUE OF A PERSON

WHAT IS THE VALUE OF A PERSON?

In many cultures men are honored more than women. Rich people are respected more than poor people. The current market value of a person is determined like the price of a car. Model, year, and condition all play a part.

The disturbing truth is that human worth, like beauty, is often in the eye of the beholder. Yet something interesting shows up in the eyes of a mother or father.

A Question of the Heart

After the birth of our son Ben in 1973 and our daughter Jen in 1979, I was overwhelmed by how much I loved both of them. At some point I remember thinking: *I'm not sure I understood the value of a person before becoming a parent.* And then another thought: *What if the devil approached me with a bid for their souls?*

Here's one way the proposition plays out. The devil offers to rig the world's largest lottery in exchange for Ben's life. Then he suggests the lifetime earnings of the world's wealthiest family in exchange for Jen. When he sees that he hasn't gotten my attention with either of these propositions, he says, "Name your price. What about all the oil in the Mideast? All the real estate in the world? All the industry on the planet? I'll throw in personal happiness, good health, and a long life for you and your wife."

You see where this is going. Your answer would be the same as mine. No amount of money or material possessions could tempt us to sell—for any price—one of our own children.

But then there is another question. What if the devil offered me all the money, real estate, and industry of the world for the soul of *someone else's* child?

Since I've just admitted that I couldn't put a price tag of any amount on one of my own children, I'm in a frame of mind to remember that everyone is somebody's baby. And by a parent's standard, there isn't another child in the world worth less than my own. Yet here my own character gives out on me. While my love for Ben and Jen tells me something about the priceless value of a person, my own conscience tells me how inconsistently I've given attention and consideration even to my own children—let alone the sons and daughters of others.

The Need for Better Eyes

There is only one Person who never lost sight of the value of every person. Day after day Jesus treated women and men, old and young, poor and rich, sick and healthy as if they all were important. Even when offered the kingdoms of the world for a moment of blind self-interest, He didn't cave in (Matthew 4:1–11). He consistently saw something in others worth dying for.

Sometimes Jesus used little things to show the value He saw in others. Once, after asking His followers to risk their lives for Him, He asked, "Are not two sparrows sold for a copper coin? And not one of them falls to the ground apart from your

Father's will. But the very hairs of your head are all numbered. Do not fear therefore; you are of more value than many sparrows" (Matthew 10:29–31). His point was clear: If the Father in heaven takes note of a sparrow falling to the ground, then imagine how much more He loves and cares for His own children.

On another occasion, Jesus used big things to show the value He sees in each person. To people inclined even to forget the value of their own life Jesus asked, "What profit is it to a man if he gains the whole world, and loses his own soul? Or what will a man give in exchange for his soul?" (Matthew 16:26).

The Eloquence of Action

Jesus' words were powerful, but His actions were even more telling. While some of the most religious people of His day looked down on or ignored women, ethnic minorities, poor people, and prisoners, Christ noticed and befriended them.

Christ's value of each person is a revolutionary principle of life. If we all shared His value of each person, our families and churches would be healthier and safer places to be. Business and industry would be transformed by owners and managers who saw workers through Christ's eyes. Nothing would give more honor and value to either our friends or our enemies than to be treated as someone "for whom Christ died" (Romans 14:15; 1 Corinthians 8:11).

The apostle John was one of Jesus' closest friends during our Lord's three years of public life, and John was deeply moved by the way Christ valued him. This love spilled over into the apostle's concern for others. In the fourth chapter of his first New Testament letter he wrote, "In this is love, not that we loved God, but that He loved us and sent His Son to be the propitiation [sacrifice] for our sins. Beloved, if God so loved us, we also ought to love one another" (1 John 4:10–11).

[101]

Father in heaven, You know how often I have treated others as if their value was to be found in their work, their appearance, or their usefulness to me. Yet, in this moment the words and sacrifice of Your Son are stirring something deep within me. I see that valuing others because of what You think of them is far more important than valuing them because of what they think of me.

By Your grace I want to be different. Please let me see through Your eyes. I want what You see in the value of a person to shape the rest of my life.

October 2002

FORGIVENESS

SOMETHING HAS GONE wrong with forgiveness. I can't tell you how often I have wandered around lately, in a mental fog, trying to figure out what forgiveness should look like in personal and national settings.

The problem shows up when people say, "I was wrong. I'm sorry. Now let's get on with business. It's your job to forgive me. It's time for us both to put this behind us."

With a few well-chosen words, the tables are turned. Like a wrestler doing an escape and reverse, an offender regains the upper hand. His victims are now expected to forgive and forget. He might even remind them that according to Jesus, if we don't forgive others, our Father in heaven won't forgive us (Matthew 6:14–15).

Is there a way to be forgiving in spirit while still helping those who have hurt us to be accountable for their actions? The answers of the Bible might surprise you.

Forgiving Doesn't Mean Forgetting

Although some wrongs are forgotten when we stop nursing them, other hurts are always near the edge of our awareness.

If we have been badly wounded, our inability to forget can cause us to feel guilty. We've been told that when God forgives, He forgets, and that if we really forgive, we'll forget too.

But God doesn't forget anything. From cover to cover, the Bible shows that God remembers the sins of His people. Both Old and New Testaments are full of stories that preserve forever the memory of His people's forgiven wrongs.

When God says He will not remember our sins, He means He won't remember them against us. He doesn't write us off or consider us worthless because of wrongs we've done. Instead, through forgiveness, He releases us from a debt we could never pay and assures us of His continuing love for us.

Forgiveness May Not Involve Complete Restoration

Those who have confessed their wrongs are likely to ask, "Now that I've admitted my wrong, now that God has forgiven me, and now that the Bible requires you to forgive me, why can't we act like this never happened?"

One answer is that forgiveness doesn't require a return to business as usual. There may be results that are irreversible. God forgave Adam and Eve, and then removed them from the Garden. God forgave the anger of Moses, but wouldn't let him into the Promised Land. God forgave David for adultery and murder, but would not let David have the child born of his adultery.

Forgiveness may allow for consequences. A forgiver may still wisely and lovingly ask for reasonable restitution, legal due process, a plan to avoid recurrences, and time to heal. Wise follow-through is often necessary if we are going to forgive and love well.

Forgiveness Doesn't Start with Us

The Bible says that the story of forgiveness begins with God. He once and for all forgives the past, present, and future sins of all who accept the cross of His Son as payment for our moral debts. He purges our record in the courts of heaven and secures forever the legal acquittal of all who trust His Son. He offers unlimited "family" forgiveness to those who continue to confess "known" sins against the Father in heaven (1 John 1:9). This second river of forgiveness washes away family issues that have brought disagreement into our relationship with the Father.

With such immeasurable forgiveness in view, Jesus tells the story of a man who was forgiven of a multimillion-dollar debt, but who turned around and refused to forgive the debt of one who owed him a relatively small amount of money (Matthew 18:21–35). Our Teacher used the story to show how immoral it is for us to take mountains of mercy from Him and then to turn around and withhold a few shovels of that mercy from those who ask us.

The message is clear. As we have received immeasurable forgiveness from God, we are to allow what we have received to overflow into the lives of those who wrong us. Jesus said to His disciples, "Take heed to yourselves. If your brother sins against you, rebuke him; and if he repents, forgive him. And if he sins against you seven times in a day, and seven times in a day returns to you, saying, 'I repent,' you shall forgive him" (Luke 17:3–4).

Forgiveness Isn't Only for Us

Because an angry, bitter spirit can be self-destructive, many believe that the ability to forgive is more for us than for the person who has hurt us. But if forgiving others is God's merciful way of helping us deal with our own bitterness, why then does He add to our pain the difficult task of confronting those who have hurt us, and to forgive them only if they say, "I repent" (Luke 17:1–4).

Jesus doesn't teach us to love our enemies and to forgive those who harm us merely to get the bitterness out of our own stomachs. Freeing ourselves of resentment is only part of what Jesus has in mind. Just as God forgives us for our sake, He asks us to join with Him in being part of the redemptive process in those who have asked for mercy. He asks us to do this not in our own strength, but by His grace working in us.

Sometimes It's Necessary to Lovingly Withhold Forgiveness

God lovingly withholds forgiveness from those who have not had a change of heart. Even though it saddens Him to do so, He will not forgive the guilt of those who knowingly refuse to admit their sin.

God's example is our wisdom. He teaches us to be saddened by the self-centeredness of others, to lovingly confront those who have wronged us, and to let His love teach us when it is in the best interests of others to extend forgiveness or to withhold it (Matthew 18:15–17; Luke 23:34).

Father in heaven, if You were to hold even one of our countless sins against us, we'd have no hope. We can hardly begin to thank You for the forgiveness You have shown us. Please help us be wise in knowing how to share that same mercy with those who hurt us. Let us do so from the embrace of Your love and from the gentle grip of Your inexpressible grace.

January 1999

SYMPHONY

OVER TIME, WE ALL COME across ideas that change the way we think about ourselves. For me, one of those thoughts is that *a well-lived life is more like a symphony than a solo.*

The point takes nothing away from a solo. I love hearing Willie Nelson sing "September Song," or Leann Rimes do her version of "Blue." A single voice performance even makes its own life lesson: *Every life is like a center-stage solo in the eyes of our Creator.* One person at a time, we are all being judged on our own act (see Romans 14:7–12).

But there is something more important than our own show. Our individual performances are part of something much greater. In the grander scheme, we aren't just here to sing our own song. All who are in Christ are members of an organization that in some ways is like a symphony orchestra.

The apostle Paul gave us a view of this bigger picture when he wrote, "For in fact the body is not one member but many. If the foot should say, 'Because I am not a hand, I am not of the body,' is it therefore not of the body? And if the ear should say, 'Because I am not an eye, I am not of the body,' is it therefore not of the body? If the whole body were an eye, where would be the hearing? If the whole were hearing, where would be the smelling? But now God has set the members, each one of them, in the body just as He pleased" (1 Corinthians 12:14–18).

The human body is like an orchestra. Individual members, important as they are, work for a purpose greater than themselves.

Shared Rhythm and Mood

Together the members of a symphony create carefully composed and orchestrated moods. Some are quiet and reflective. Others build with great energy and resolve with a flourish. At the direction of their conductor, the members of a well-rehearsed orchestra move as one.

In the wisdom of God, the members of the body of Christ are also designed to resonate and move with one another. When one hurts, those who care share the pain. When one does well, the love of friends and family gives many reasons to be happy (1 Corinthians 12:25–27). With such resonance and rhythm in view, the apostle Paul urged members of God's family, "Rejoice with those who rejoice, and weep with those who weep" (Romans 12:15).

When the people of Christ care for one another, they move like the rising and falling emotions of a symphony. This is by our great Composer's design. As explained by the lyrically beautiful yet profound words of Solomon: "To everything there is a season, a time for every purpose under heaven: a time to be born, and a time to die; . . . a time to kill, and a time to heal; a time to break down, and a time to build up; a time to weep, and a time to laugh; a time to mourn, and a time to dance; . . . a time to keep silence, and a time to speak; a time to love, and a time to hate; a time of war, and a time of peace" (Ecclesiastes 3:1–4, 7–8).

Tonal Blend and Variation

To produce contrasting moods and grand sweeps of symphonic harmony a well-trained orchestra moves together through complex notes, chords, scores, rests. So, too, the music of God is heard not only in the cooperation of many people, but also in the blending of many spiritual notes, facts, and principles:

The *Ten Commandments of the Mosaic covenant* combined to define the boundaries of moral behavior (Exodus 20:1–17).

The *nine character traits of the new covenant* blend to show what a Spirit-filled follower of Christ looks like (Galatians 5:22–23).

The *seven attitudes taught by Christ* merge to describe the making of a peacemaker (Matthew 5:1–10).

The *seven progressive expressions of due diligence* show that faith works through and in harmony with the essentials of spiritual growth (2 Peter 1:5–7).

The *seven marks of spirituality* help us recognize the wisdom that comes from God with balance and depth (James 3:17).

The *fifteen characteristics of real love* help us to be sure that our affections and behavior are as loving as we want them to be (1 Corinthians 13).

The *seven pieces of spiritual armor* show us why it's dangerous to think that being in Christ automatically protects us from spiritual attack and failure (Ephesians 6:10–18).

Every word and principle of God stands on its own, but not alone. Without truth, faith is presumption. Without patience, hope is impulsive. Without love, eloquence is noise (1 Corinthians 13:1).

The Conductor

Without a director, the members of an orchestra could all be playing their own song. Even in the same symphony they could be on different pages.

So, too, the people of Christ need a great Director who can turn their individual contributions into shared music. With the music of many voices in mind, the apostle Paul wrote to the Colossians, "Let the word of Christ dwell in you richly in all wisdom, teaching and admonishing one another in psalms and hymns and spiritual songs, singing with grace in your hearts to the Lord. And whatever you do in word or deed, do all in the name of the Lord Jesus, giving thanks to God the Father through Him" (Colossians 3:16–17).

Without the leadership of Christ, we would be left looking for a leader worthy of our complete confidence. Apart from His direction, the church would be little more than a group of individuals stumbling through a piece of music no one really understands.

Yet, in the noise of our individual lives, Christ stands among us, ready to be our great Conductor. The composition is His. The music is His. And the orchestra, conceived and bought at great price, is also His. Together we are rehearsing for a presentation far greater than any of us have yet imagined.

Father in heaven, in our quiet moments we hear the sounds of a great symphony in the distance. Forgive us for thinking that our one-person performance is all that counts. Please help us not to miss our part in the greater symphony—no matter how much or little You ask of us.

May 2004

A HEARTACHE

Dear Chris,

The last time we talked, you asked whether I thought those who end their own lives could go to heaven. Since we didn't get a chance to finish that conversation, I hope you don't mind if I use this letter to say some things that I wish I'd been able to say at the time.

I responded to your question by saying something like, "Yes, those who take their own lives can go to heaven. Our last choice in this life does not determine where we go after death." But then I hesitated, and asked why you were wondering. When you looked away and said, "Not now," I heard the emotion in your voice and sensed that you needed some space.

A mutual friend has since told me about your heartache. I've learned about the loss of your son—and your uncertainty about where he was in his spiritual journey.

Your inability to talk about your loss is something I haven't been able to forget. As I've replayed the moment, I've realized that you weren't the only one who wasn't ready to talk. Now I'm glad that I didn't say something I thought would make you feel better. That would have been a mistake. I'm quite sure you were not looking for false assurance any more than you were looking for someone to tell you how you should be feeling.

Chris, I'm not writing to tell you more than I know. You know as well as I do that God alone understands the state of mind of those who end their own lives. He alone understands their pain and their confusion. He alone knows how to give comfort and courage to those who remain.

So why am I writing? I'm writing because I don't want you to be surprised if you find yourself wanting to avoid religious people, the church, the Bible, or even God Himself. Emotional pain can put distance between ourselves and others. And there is no way to sort through our feelings quickly—especially in the middle of a heartbreaking loss.

God doesn't want us to ignore our grief. What is happening to you right now is not something you can afford to deny. Even though David of the Bible was a man after God's own heart, he spent long days and nights with his losses, his fears, his regrets—and his anger.

I also believe that if it were possible for you to meet face to face with the most compassionate Person who ever lived, you would not hear religious answers that told you how to feel. He wouldn't condemn you for the waves of anger you feel toward heaven, yourself, or even your son, for leaving you in such agony. My guess is that He would put His arm around your shoulder and cry with you.

I admit that I don't know what this merciful and honest Person would say to you. He was always so unpredictable. Not in a bad way, but with wisdom and understanding. He had a way of saying what His friends and enemies didn't expect Him to say. He knew more about pain and evil than anyone else around Him—yet He didn't teach His followers to wave their fists against heaven and to curse the darkness.

Chris, I believe we can learn a lot by thinking about the cursing He didn't do, the battles against heaven He didn't fight, and the despair He overcame. Even though He loved so deeply, He didn't go mad out of His concern for others.

No, we can't live with the same spiritual awareness that He had. Neither can we expect each other to trust heaven as implicitly as He did. What we can do, though, is remind one another that even Jesus cried out at the lowest point in His life, "My God, My God, why have You forsaken Me?"

When the Son of God left heaven to become the Son of Man, He voluntarily laid aside the boundless understanding that He shared with His Father. And when, in the dark corridors of human experience, He walked into a house of mourning, He cried. As He approached moments of separation from those He loved the most, He sweated and struggled in great agony before saying, "Nevertheless not My will, but Yours be done." In all these ways He showed that trusting the unseen hand of God is not just an event but a learned process.

It is when our broken hearts drive us to the place where we wonder if we can continue that we have every reason to cling to the One who loves better than we do. He is the One who says, "Come to Me, all you who are weary and burdened, and I will give you rest."

Chris, please forgive me if I have in any way added to your pain. I want so much for you to find the strength and comfort that can only be explained by God's love for you.

Sincerely,
Mart

October 2000

A PERSONAL LOSS

Dear Al,

The last time we talked, you asked a question I couldn't answer. I remember the concern in your eyes and how helpless I felt to give you any assurance when you asked, "Does the Bible offer any comfort when we're afraid someone we love has died without Christ?"

Your heartbreak is understandable. So is your anger. I can see why you feel that your faith has turned against you. Beliefs that once gave you comfort are now robbing you of sleep.

Other questions you asked have also been hounding me. Why didn't our Lord help us with such an important issue? Why did the apostle Paul write as if his readers are concerned only about loved ones who "die in the Lord" (1 Thessalonians 4:15–17)? Didn't he realize the impact his words would have on those who, because of their faith, would agonize even more deeply because they would have no hope of ever again seeing someone they love so much?

Your questions caught me off guard. But the longer I have thought about them, the more convinced I've become that even in our concern for unsaved loved ones we do not grieve as those "who have no hope."

There Is a Time to Comfort

As there is a time to warn, so there is a time to console. That comfort goes beyond our Lord's assurance that He will some-day wipe all tears from our eyes (Revelation 21:4). We can also find consolation knowing that it is none other than Jesus who will judge all of the earth (John 5:26–27). Because of the concern He showed for people during His life on earth, we can be sure He cares more about our lost loved ones than we do.

We see a hint of that compassion when Jesus mourned the unbelief of those who rejected Him (Matthew 23:37). We hear Him teaching His disciples to love their enemies (Luke 6:35). And in the moment of His deepest suffering, we hear Him say of those who called for His death, "Father, forgive them, for they do not know what they do" (Luke 23:34).

Ever since coming to know Christ, those of us who believe in Him have been learning to rely on Him more than on ourselves. We've been discovering that we can trust His goodness more than our own fears.

While believing that everything Jesus said about heaven and hell is true, we can cling to the truth that both mercy and justice have their origin in Him. The God whom Christ personified is not cruel. He will not add unnecessary pain to the fate of those who die rejecting Him. The suffering of judgment will be neither more nor less than it needs to be.

What We Don't Know

We don't know how our Lord will give "many stripes" (lashes of judgment) to some and "few stripes" to others (Luke 12:47–48), except that the punishment of some will be as severe as the punishment of others will be light. We don't know the full meaning of the fire and darkness of judgment, except that the Hebrew prophet Isaiah first used the language of everlasting fire and smoke as a way of describing a battlefield defeat that is final and irreversible (Isaiah 34:9–10; 66:24).

What We Do Know

What we do know is that God will be fair, and good, and right in judgment. We know that not all will experience the same degree of pain and regret. All will be judged according to their works, which is one reason my grandfather Dr. M. R. De Haan said repeatedly, "To some, hell will be a little heaven compared to what it will be for others."

The Scriptures show that those who suffer the severest judgment will be the devil, the Antichrist, the False Prophet, and those who accept the mark of the beast in the last days (Revelation 14:11; 20:10). In a similar way, Jesus reserved His strongest warnings for those religious leaders who used their influence to turn the crowds against Him.

There Is a Time to Grieve

The apostle Paul grieved for lost loved ones without losing his mind or faith. He cared so much for Jewish family members that he would have taken their place in judgment if he could have. He said, "I have great sorrow and continual grief in my heart. For I could wish that I myself were accursed from Christ for my brethren, my countrymen according to the flesh" (Romans 9:2–3). Yet Paul's concern for others didn't rob him of his affection for heaven or his confidence in Christ (Philippians 1:23–24).

There Is a Time to Rest

We cannot afford to let fear of what we don't know about the future rob us of what we do know about our Savior and Lord. There is no better person to trust with the souls of our lost loved ones. He alone is their judge. He alone understands all of the factors that make faith and character more difficult for some than for others.

Most of our fears for those who have died lie not in what Jesus said, but in what we add by our own imagination. This is where we need to doubt ourselves and trust that even as He judges our lost loved ones the Lord will give us reason to worship and love Him forever.

Al, with you in mind, I bow my knees and pray, "Father, in heaven, at the end of our own fears, and at the end of our own wits, we cast ourselves upon You. We take comfort in the fact that You take no joy in the death of lost people. We cling to the assurance that You, our Father, the Judge of all the earth, will do right."

June 2001

AN ADMISSION

THIS IS AN OPEN LETTER addressed to someone who exists in the collective experience of people I've had the privilege of knowing and learning from over the years.

Dear Aaron,

I hope you are doing well. I miss our conversations about life, religion, and the Chicago Cubs. Even more, I regret that we haven't kept in touch after your move to Philadelphia.

I'm writing now because time has changed my thoughts on a subject we used to disagree about, and I owe you an update.

Aaron, you used to say that "Church people aren't better than anyone else; they just think they are. The best people I know never darken the door of a church."

Even though I argued with you at the time, you helped me see that people who build hospitals, orphanages, and rescue missions in the name of Christ aren't the only ones working for the benefit of humanity. I remember the "letters to the editor" you wrote, and the streets you walked, to protest the wrongs of racism, the evils of war, and the pollution of the environment.

Since the last time we talked, I've traveled enough internationally to see the hospitality and goodwill of people of non-Christian cultures. In other countries, as in our own, I've seen that a person doesn't have to believe in Christ to be loving, gracious, and even heroic in the face of human need.

Such experiences over the years have reminded me of the disbelief I saw in your eyes when I talked to you about becoming "a new person in Christ." I remember the questions you asked when I quoted the words of the apostle Paul, "If anyone is in Christ, he is a new creation; old things have passed away; behold, all things have become new." You told me you didn't buy it, that you had grown up in the church and knew firsthand that these were not people for whom all things had become new.

Well, Aaron, enough time has passed that I am able to understand more clearly what you were saying. Along the way I've seen enough in myself and in others to give me second thoughts about what I said to you. Somewhere along the line I started asking questions: If believing in Christ changes people's hearts—why are His followers unable to sustain the "first love" and enthusiasm of their relationship with Christ? Why do so many eventually struggle with personal bitterness, church conflict, troubled marriages, investment scandals, anxiety disorders, and a whole spectrum of addictive behaviors? Why does faith in Christ produce changes that are more like the honeymoon phase of a marriage than a lasting change in life?

At this point, I admit that my spiritual journey has run parallel to what I've learned in marriage. What doesn't change in either is the human baggage we bring into both. The independent inclinations that were a part of me before and after marriage were also a part of me before and after I put my faith in Christ. The self-centeredness that makes it difficult for me to hear the concerns of my wife also makes it hard for me to hear the voice of Christ living in me. It took time for me to discover that in salvation and in marriage, growth and maturity do not come automatically or easily. In both cases, I was not prepared for what turned out to be the greatest challenges of my life. What I didn't realize beforehand is that the biggest enemy I would ever face would be my own unchanged inclination toward self-centeredness.

I don't mean to understate all the wonderful sides of marriage or conversion. But I can see now how wrong my expectations were. I had looked to salvation to make me good, as I had looked to marriage to make me happy. I didn't see that in both cases my own human nature would stack the deck against me if I didn't do whatever it took to let the Spirit of Christ live His life in me.

Aaron, as I look back on some of our conversations, it's clear that I was wrong in assuming that my whole life had changed through faith in Christ. It didn't occur to me that whenever the Bible encourages us to love, or to pray, or to think and speak honestly, it is because we are so inclined to do just the opposite.

Yes, Aaron, my thinking has changed a lot since the last time we talked. Life has been a lot harder than I expected. Too often I have underestimated the diligence needed to let Christ make a difference in me.

I can now see more clearly that upon a couple's public confession, a minister declares a man and woman married, but not mature. And, upon an individual's faith in Christ, God declares us righteous in Christ, but not good in ourselves. In both cases there is a huge difference between the legal declaration and resulting quality of life.

I now believe that church people, in their best moments, have a lot in common with members of a twelve-step recovery group. They attend meetings and work the program, not because they are better than others but because they know they need God and one another to overcome the problems that would ruin their lives.

I only wish, Aaron, that I had understood years ago why so many people like me reflect far more of ourselves than of who we are, and could be, in Him.

Thanks for listening. I'd love to know where you are in your own spiritual journey. If you are inclined, drop me a line, either by letter or e-mail. I hope you'll find that I'm more ready to listen and less likely to defend the moral superiority of anyone other than the One who died for us.

Sincerely,
Mart

October 2004

MENTAL HEALTH

SOON AFTER OUR MARRIAGE, my wife and I were faced with the needs of a family member whose inner world was deeply troubled.

Sometimes this loved one heard voices no one else could hear. Sometimes she had fears that the government was spying on her through her television set. Sometimes she accused us of trying to kill her.

For a while she lived in our home. On other occasions she was able to care for herself in government-subsidized housing. More than once she ran away in an attempt to avoid a world that frightened her.

With the help of local mental health services, we did everything we knew how to do. Through it all, we loved and laughed and prayed. Sometimes she went to church with us. One Sunday evening, she expressed a desire to accept Christ as her Savior. For a while, her state of mind improved. But within a few months the voices and hallucinations returned, and eventually her troubled life ended in a state hospital.

Over time, we developed a deep appreciation for the doctors, mental health community, and social workers who helped us. On occasion, we needed the help of law enforcement officers and judges to obtain involuntary admission to a mental health facility, or we needed the oversight of a financial conservator.

We also became aware of other church and neighborhood families who were dealing with similar heartbreak. They too were praying for spiritual help, while reading mental health literature for medical answers.

Along the way, we saw why doctors often refer their patients to counselors and why counselors refer their patients to doctors. The human body and mind are so interwoven that physical symptoms can mask spiritual problems, just as emotional and mental confusion can obscure organic causes.

Like the body, the mind sometimes heals itself. Sometimes it doesn't. Often there is a place for medication to provide relief while wise counselors offer perspective and new ways of dealing with confused thoughts. There's a time for both doctors and counselors. Persons struggling with mental health issues may respond to either, to both, or to neither. Sometimes the pain is softened only by sedation.

Such complexity calls for wisdom so that we can offer spiritual answers with gentleness rather than presumption. Jesus' offer of forgiveness, love, and truth provides a foundation for good mental health. Many have found their inner world of anxiety and hopelessness calmed and strengthened by personal faith through reading the Bible. Some have a story that is similar to those who have found deliverance from spiritual oppression in the presence of Jesus. Prayer in Jesus' name should not be ruled out. But our humility needs to be as real as our faith. There are countless people who suffer from depressive and compulsive thinking that does not respond to prayer, Bible reading, or spiritual correction.

On more than a few occasions I've been deeply troubled by the apparent unwillingness of God to answer prayers for those who live in such inner confusion and anguish. I see families who are barely surviving in their effort to care for loved ones tormented by autism, Alzheimer's, or other conditions that affect not only the body but the mind and emotions as well. But then, in the face of such brokenness, I'm reminded that the Bible doesn't ask us to believe in a God who fixes everything in this life.

Those of us who believe that the Bible is all we need to treat mental and emotional problems usually allow for exceptions rooted in organic causes. We recognize that we must leave room for thoughts and emotions altered by the real effects of brain cancer, thyroid disease, or chemotherapy. What we sometimes forget, though, is that bodies and minds that are fearfully and wonderfully made can be tearfully and woefully broken.

Mental and emotional health and illness are a matter of degree. No one but God fully understands the complex interplay between body and mind.

We might wish that life were simple enough to say, "Think right, do right, and you'll feel right." While such advice works for some people some of the time, it can add even more pain to those who are already hurting the most. The apostle Paul gives us a more thoughtful approach when he writes, "Warn those who are unruly, comfort the fainthearted, uphold the weak, be patient with all" (1 Thessalonians 5:14).

Note the varied responses. Warn some. Comfort some. Hold up some. Be patient toward all.

The need for such patience is easy to see in a child or adult struggling with profound mental or emotional impairment. In such cases, we are inspired by the gentleness and patience of a caregiver who loves in ways that are not returned. We wonder at the compassion that tenderly makes room for limitation while always looking for undeveloped potential.

But it's important to see that Paul's words are not just addressed to those with obvious impairment, or even with the kind of diagnosed schizophrenia that my wife and I saw in our loved one. Paul urges, "Be patient with all."

All of us live with a complexity that is not easily understood by others or ourselves. This is one of many reasons the Bible encourages us to relate to others with a spirit of thoughtful patience and firm gentleness rather than with a spirit of judgment and condemnation. If we are followers of Jesus, filled with His Spirit, we will be more than moral drill sergeants. Guided by His Spirit, we will give others the consideration we want for ourselves.

If troubled people need our help, we don't do them a favor by ignoring or indulging unhealthy thinking when there is reason to believe they could be making better choices. Love needs to be strong, and sometimes even tough, in dealing with those who are profoundly impaired. But this is where we need to use wisdom and patience rather than the presumption of ignorance.

Father in heaven, there is so much we don't understand about others and ourselves. Please help us to know when to warn, when to comfort, when to hold up, while being patient toward all.

December 2006

FORGIVING OURSELVES

WHY DO WE PUNISH OURSELVES for old regrets long after we believe God has forgiven us? This question stuck in my mind after a conversation with someone I'll call TC. TC described himself as being in recovery for multiple addictions. A couple of times he said, "My problem was forgiving myself. I found it a lot easier to believe God had forgiven me than to forgive myself for what I'd done."

In some ways I knew what TC was talking about. Long after believing God had forgiven me, I have silently cursed myself for doing things that embarrassed me and hurt others. What unnerved me is that TC seemed more willing than I was to admit that forgiving ourselves is something we need to do.

Is it up to us to forgive ourselves? Although I was willing to beat myself up for past wrongs, offering mercy to myself seemed like playing God. If God wants us to pardon ourselves, I wondered why the Bible doesn't quote Him as saying something like, "Even as I have released you from guilt, so you must now release yourselves."

What surprised me is that TC helped me see that, without realizing it, I was doing the very thing I thought I was trying to avoid. He said, "I have a friend who got on my case for acting like I was greater than God. This friend kept saying, 'Who do you think you are, God Almighty? God forgives you. But you don't. What is this you're telling me? Are you greater than God?'"

The good-natured prodding TC took from his friend helped me. Later, I remembered words of the apostle John who wrote in his first New Testament letter: "This then is how we know that we belong to the truth, and how we *set our hearts at rest* in his presence *whenever our hearts condemn us.* For God is greater than our hearts, and he knows everything" (1 John 3:19–20 NIV, emphasis added).

Why is it important to remember that God is greater than our hearts? John reminded us that when the sin we have already confessed continues to torment us, God sees more clearly than we do. He sees everything. He sees the wrong and the regret we have acknowledged. He sees the price He has paid to release us from that sin. He sees the trust we have put in His Son. He sees the good work He has started in our hearts. And He knows that what He has begun He will finish (Philippians 1:6).

God also sees something else. He sees the people around us who are negatively affected as long as we continue to condemn ourselves. He knows we will never be good at loving others as long as we refuse to let the love and forgiveness of God flush the guilt and shame out of our lives.

Just before raising the problem of self-condemnation, John wrote, "This is how we know what love is: Jesus Christ laid down his life for us. And we ought to lay down our lives for our brothers. If anyone has material possessions and sees his brother in need but has no pity on him, how can the love of God be in him?" (1 John 3:16–17 NIV).

John's question prompts another. How can the love of God flow through us to those around us if we are saying, in effect, "I know You have forgiven me, Lord, but I have higher standards and expectations for myself than You do. I can't walk with You. I can't join You in Your mission of love, because I haven't lived up to my own expectations." We may think that's humility, but it's probably wounded pride.

What does lingering guilt tell us about ourselves?

We may be expecting too much of ourselves. Whether we are struggling with our own wounded pride or grieving what we have lost, God's thoughts are more reassuring than our own. Psalm 103 says, "He has not dealt with us according to our sins, nor punished us according to our iniquities. For as the heavens are high above the earth, so great is His mercy toward those who fear Him; as far as the east is from the west, so far has He removed our transgressions from us. As a father pities his children, so the Lord pities those who fear Him. For He knows our frame; He remembers that we are dust" (Psalm 103:10–14).

We may be limiting our ability to be what God wants us to be. Refusing to forgive ourselves as God has forgiven us does nothing but prolong and multiply our sin. Self-condemnation is the opposite of the gratitude that opens our hearts to God.

Open hearts to God and others is what the apostle John had in mind when he went on to write: "Dear friends, if our hearts do not condemn us, we have confidence before God and receive from him anything we ask, because we obey his commands and do what pleases him. And this is his command: to believe in the name of his Son, Jesus Christ, and to love one another as he commanded us. Those who obey his commands live in him, and he in them. And this is how we know that he lives in us: We know it by the Spirit he gave us" (1 John 3:21–24 NIV).

Every day of self-absorbed self-condemnation is a day spent robbing ourselves of the joy of a grateful heart. Every hour of beating ourselves up is an hour spent robbing others of the good that God wants to do for them through us. By contrast, every day lived in the freedom of forgiveness is a day spent praising God. Every hour lived in gratitude for forgiveness is a day spent loving others on God's behalf.

Father in heaven, in our thoughtful moments we know You are greater than our hearts. You see infinitely more than we do. You see the work You have begun in us, the Spirit You have given us, the forgiveness You have bought for us, and the desire You have given us to live in freedom rather than to hide behind past failures. Please help us to use that freedom to love others as You have first loved us.

June 2003

INFORMATION OVERLOAD

NEVER BEFORE HAVE SO MANY had access to so much information. With human knowledge doubling every few years and search engines like Google, Alta Vista, and Ask Jeeves at our fingertips, the potential for learning seems endless.

Ironically, much of what we are discovering helps us to see how little we know. According to Reuters News Service, the Hubble Space Telescope has seen 10,000 galaxies in a window of the night sky about the size of a full moon. Who can even begin to imagine what it means to find 10,000 *galaxies* in one small area of the heavens? Our own galaxy, the Milky Way, is made up of about 100 *billion* stars, and our whole solar system revolves around only *one* of them.

The Promise of Knowledge

The Human Genome Project is another scientific effort that is harvesting knowledge faster than our minds can process. This global effort to map and sequence all of the 100,000 genes of the human body promises hopeful and disturbing implications for the treatment and prevention of disease. Deciphering the DNA alphabet of the human body brings with it the possibility of human clones to donate organs and gain complete knowledge of the human genetic code, so that any human characteristic can be altered with minimal risk or error. But who can understand the real benefits and risks of having this kind of knowledge?

The Danger of Knowledge

As with everything else in life, there is a downside to living on an information highway. Overloaded computers can crash and our minds can lock up. While looking for useful knowledge, we can get lost in a blinding blizzard of data. The same browsers we are using to solve our problems can be used to look for world-class gossip, pornography, or instructions on how to make a bomb.

Our Need for Wisdom

Our first parents discovered long ago that knowledge without wisdom is dangerous. By eating from the tree of the knowledge of good and evil they made the fatal mistake of trying to match wits with their Creator.

From that day until now, infected knowledge has been to the human mind what corrupted files are to our computers. Like the MyDoom virus that did billions of dollars of damage by clogging information systems with unwanted e-mails, so the pursuit of knowledge without wisdom can overload our minds and drown us in data.

The Meaning of Wisdom

Wisdom is the practical side of knowledge. It shows us what is important, gives proportion to what we know, and enables us to use insight skillfully to reach a desired goal.

There is more than one kind of wisdom. According to the New Testament, the wisdom of the world is different than the wisdom of God. The first uses knowledge to get ahead at the expense of others. The second uses understanding for the good of others. Each is distinguished by its motives.

Seeing that real wisdom is not only a function of the mind but also a condition of the heart, James, an apostle of Christ, wrote: "Who is wise and understanding among you? Let him show by good conduct that his works are done in the meekness of wisdom. For where envy and self-seeking exist, confusion and every evil thing are there. But the wisdom that is from above is first pure, then peaceable, gentle, willing to yield, full of mercy and good fruits, without partiality and without hypocrisy. Now the fruit of righteousness is sown in peace by those who make peace" (James 3:13, 16–18).

By describing what's at the heart of both kinds of wisdom, James explained why knowledge makes some people arrogant while enabling others to love. The wisdom he recommended is "pure" because it is not infected with "selfish ambition." It is "peaceable" because it values good relationships with others. It is "gentle" because it knows the value of handling others with care. This wisdom is "willing to yield" and is "full of mercy and good fruits." It is also "without partiality and without hypocrisy" because it puts the well-being of others above selfish interests.

The Source of Real Wisdom

Once we see that knowledge without wisdom is like marriage without love, we can see why Solomon wrote, "Happy is the [person] who finds wisdom, and the man [or woman] who gains understanding; for her proceeds are better than the profits of silver, and her gain than fine gold. She is more precious than rubies, and all the things you may desire cannot compare with her" (Proverbs 3:13–15).

The priceless treasure Solomon is describing is found by those who invest their lives in the principles of the Bible. The Old Testament describes a wisdom that begins with the fear of God and is rounded out by timeless principles of practical insight (Proverbs 1:1–7; 9:10). The New Testament builds on the wisdom of Moses and Solomon but moves to another level of enlightenment. With the coming of Christ, the Gospel writers introduce us to someone who makes the wisdom of Solomon pale by comparison. As the Son of God, Jesus did more than teach truth and knowledge and wisdom. He personified it (1 Corinthians 1:20–31).

As Lord of heaven and earth, Jesus could have overwhelmed us with new information. He could have lectured on science, theology, and philosophy in the most prestigious academies of higher learning. Yet when He walked among us, He talked about what He knew was most important. He talked about honoring His Father and seeing the value of people who were regarded as worthless by others.

Showing wisdom with a heart of love, Jesus had a way of putting other information in perspective. With a wisdom that speaks for itself, He simply asked questions like, "What profit is it to a man if he gains the whole world, and loses his own soul? Or what will a man give in exchange for his soul?" (Matthew 16:26).

Father, in heaven, we are so quickly distracted from what is important. In our knowledge we are so inclined to be proud and self-sufficient. Please renew us once again in the knowledge and wisdom and love of Your Son.

June 2004

TEN THINGS I LEARNED FROM MY DAD

IN THE MEMORIES THAT COME with a parent's passing, I've been reminded of what my dad taught those of us who lived and worked with him.*

In many ways, Dad didn't have an easy life. Long before his problems with a detached retina, heart surgery, and Parkinson's disease, he lived in the shadow of his own father's colorful and commanding personality. While most people knew Dad as a strong-voiced, caring, and faithful teacher of the Bible, those of us who were close to him know that along the way he also wrestled with serious and deep questions about his own abilities and self-worth.

Looking back, I'm beginning to realize how much he taught us not only by his strengths but also by the way he responded

---

* My father, Richard W. De Haan, served RBC Ministries in various capacities throughout his life. He led RBC from 1965 to 1985, when he stepped down because of health issues. I wrote this after his death in 2002.

to his weaknesses. I know my three brothers would agree that Dad showed us how to:

Admit when we are wrong. We all remember Dad's willingness to admit his faults. I'm not sure why that seems important enough to mention first. It could be that I've heard my wife Di talk about how that quality impressed her. When visiting in our home before we were married, she saw Dad come to the dinner table and, before sitting down, apologize to the family for his irritability toward Mom. Or, maybe I just can't think of anything that continues to be more necessary for me than to admit my own wrongs.

Don't try to be someone else. Dad knew what it was like to be compared to his gifted and much-loved father. Some told him he didn't have what it would take to lead the ministry his father founded. The comparisons were hard on him. But over time he used the experience to show us how to be the person God made us to be. And as a result of what he found in the trenches of his own battle for self-respect, he gave the rest of us the freedom we needed to be ourselves as well.

Think small while dreaming big. Dad showed us the importance of being honest in little things. He'd go back to a restaurant to return change if he found he'd been given too much at the cash register. What others called "white lies" were big issues to him. He didn't even like to exaggerate to make a point. For him, issues of urgency or cost were no excuse to forget the principle that "he who is faithful in what is least is faithful also in much" (Luke 16:10). Attention to detail, however, didn't keep him from dreaming. His vision for outreach through television and multiple teachers resulted in years of growth of RBC Ministries.

Be careful what we say about others. Dad wasn't part of "the grapevine" that circulates news of other people's failures. I don't remember hearing him talk about other leaders' mistakes. Maybe it was because he himself had felt the sting of unkind rumors and remarks. He simply took to heart the Scriptures that call us to love one another. The thirteenth chapter of 1 Corinthians was one of Dad's favorite Scripture passages, and he read it often to his staff.

Read biographies with a grain of salt. Dad's reluctance to be unnecessarily critical of others came with an interesting footnote. He didn't put a lot of stock in biographies. Although he saw the value of "stories of great people," he took them with a grain of salt. He knew that the real story of a person's life is seldom published.

Relax with those who are important to you. Dad worked hard. While taking his leadership responsibilities seriously, he wrote, edited, and rewrote his messages and devotionals until they had the simplicity and clarity he was looking for. But he also knew how to put his work aside and relax. He loved walks on the beach or going for a drive in the country with Mom. He looked forward to spending time on the golf course with friends. I remember how much he enjoyed showing my brothers and me how to use a fly rod to work an orange spider into the lily pads of a quiet lake as we hunted for bluegill or largemouth bass. We also have plenty of memories of him at home with a bowl of popcorn and a board game like Monopoly or Scrabble.

Cultivate balance. Dad learned by experience to listen to both sides of an argument. In his later years he told us how, as a young manager, he'd listen to one side of an employee conflict and think he understood the problem. Then he'd talk to the other side and hear a completely different perspective. The balance and fairness he cultivated in employee relationships showed up in other ways too. In so many ways he taught us to avoid one-sided extremes in thinking or behavior.

Avoid irreverent jokes. Over the years we saw in Dad a healthy fear of the Lord. Jokes about the Scripture were out of bounds as far as he was concerned. It wasn't that he didn't have a sense of humor. He loved a good laugh. But he drew the line when it came to talking lightly about God or the Bible.

Question our own use of Scripture. Because of Dad's reverence for the Word of God, he also taught us to second-guess the way we quote the Bible. When critiquing manuscripts written by his staff, he would repeatedly write in the margin, "Does the Bible really say that? Really?" He showed us that if we really want to trust or teach what God has said, we need to be willing to doubt our own interpretations and motives.

Trust in God and do the right. Since Dad's passing many of his friends, co-workers, and family members have agreed on one central focus that seems to best represent his life. Much of the legacy he left us can be summed up in the words, "Trust in God and do the right." We remember those words as they are repeated in a poem written by Norman Macleod that Dad often read to his staff.

Trust in God
by Norman Macleod

Courage, Brother, do not stumble,
Though your path be dark as night;
There's a star to guide the humble,
Trust in God and do the right.

Let the road be rough and dreary,
And its end far out of sight,

Foot it bravely, strong or weary;
Trust in God and do the right.

Perish policy and cunning,
Perish all that fears the light;
Whether losing, whether winning,
Trust in God and do the right.

Trust no party, sect or faction,
Trust no leaders in the fight;
But in every word and action
Trust in God and do the right.

Simple rule and safest guiding,
Inward peace and inward might,
Star upon our path abiding;
Trust in God and do the right.

Some will hate you, some will love you,
Some will flatter, some will slight;
Cease from man, and look above you,
Trust in God and do the right.

December 2002

THE TRUST CARD

FOR THOSE WHO'VE KNOWN the emotions and betrayals of conflict, the words are familiar: "I can't forget what happened. I don't trust you anymore, and I'm not sure I can ever trust you again." Those words are like a trump card. Whoever plays it wins the hand. It doesn't matter what cards the other player is holding. They are now useless. That's how it feels to a person who hears the words, "I'm sorry. I can't help it. I can't make myself trust you. Anything you say or do now isn't going to change the way I feel."

Mutual trust is so important to healthy relationships that its value might seem impossible to over-emphasize.

Yet we also need to be realistic. In one way or another we all lose trust in others, and at one time or another others invariably lose trust in us. Either way, as difficult as the experience is, we need to keep in mind that a loss of trust between family members, co-workers, or friends is not the end of the world.

But what can we do when we lose trust in others, or when others lose trust in us? If you're working through these kinds of issues, I hope one or more of the following thoughts will help you take the next step in what may be a long and difficult road.

Don't deny the pain of lost trust. The Bible itself says, "Confidence in an unfaithful man in time of trouble is like a bad tooth, and a foot out of joint" (Proverbs 25:19). We don't need to beat ourselves up or act as if something's wrong with us if we can't lovingly overlook the damages of unfaithfulness.

Trust needs to be earned. When we let others down, the Scriptures teach us to admit the damage we have done to others and to take action that confirms our change of heart. Yet we need to realize that even if forgiveness is granted, we cannot wipe away the consequences of a shattered trust merely by saying, "I was wrong. I'm sorry. Will you forgive me?" As important as words are to express regret and change of heart, words alone are not enough to renew trust. Depending on the severity of the offense, it may take days, months, or years of faithful behavior to restore a betrayed confidence.

At the same time, if we are the one who has been let down, we may need to realize that through this devastating experience we have learned an important lesson.

Our trust needs to be in God. The Bible might not say what we think it says about trusting others. I discovered this when I reached for my computer and began punching search commands into Bible software.

The results of my search surprised me. While the Bible emphasizes the importance of being trustworthy, I could not find one direct statement saying that we are to trust one another. On the contrary, over and over the Bible tells us not to trust people; that cursed is the one who puts his trust in man; and that God alone is to be trusted (Psalm 146:3; Proverbs 29:25; Jeremiah 17:5, 7). The Scriptures make it clear that when our deepest reliance is in ourselves or in others, we are ripe for disappointment and even despair. God alone can be counted on, not only to keep all His promises but to be all we need long after everyone else is gone.

The Bible shows us how to treat those who don't deserve our trust. Just about the time I am sure that trust is something I give only to those who earn it, I read 1 Corinthians 13, which seems to call for some level of trust whether it's deserved or not. Paul said, "[Love] always protects, always trusts, always hopes, always perseveres" (1 Corinthians 13:7 NIV).

Does this mean we should trust a convicted embezzler with our money or a suspected child molester with our children? No. Love doesn't offer trust that enables an offender to re-offend. Wise love will not feel compelled to entrust ever again such a person with our money or children. But what love can do is extend the kind of trust that allows others to prove that their confession, regret, and repentance are real. Love can extend the kind of trust that recognizes what God can do in a repentant heart. When repentance is real, the person will not demand the same privileges and freedom he or she enjoyed before breaking trust. A person with a heart being changed by God is willing to be held accountable, to slowly and purposefully give others reason to re-establish some level of trust. When people who break trust are unwilling to restore it slowly, or if they accept limited trust as an expression of distrust or even an insult, they give us good reason to believe that they have not had a real change of heart.

God wants to live this kind of love through us. I'm convinced that it is only as we learn to rely on God as our provider and protector that we will be able to entrust to others our time, our prayers, and the appropriate expressions of friendship. It is only as we personally find Him trustworthy and faithful that we can find something better than an "I'll never trust you again" attitude. With a deep confidence in God alone, we don't have to play the trust card or the vengeance card the way we are inclined to play them.

If life is likened to a game of cards, there is more in our hand than the trust card. There is also the truth card, the wisdom card, the consequences card, the love card, the mutual accountability card, the Spirit card, the trust-in-God card, the forgiveness card, and the time card.

Father, please help us to learn from Your Son. We know that it was only because He trusted You that He was able to entrust Himself, His life, and His mission to us. Please enable us by Your grace and Spirit to live in His likeness. Show us how to trust You above all so that we can take the risks of lovingly entrusting ourselves to one another.

December 1999

UNFAIRNESS

LIFE ISN'T FAIR. Good things happen to those who don't deserve them. Terrible things happen to some of the most wonderful people. Helpless children suffer for their parents' mistakes. Some who work hard are cut down prematurely by accident or disease. Others who hardly work inherit the wealth of someone else's sacrifice. Nothing under the sun is equal. Time and chance seem to happen to all (Ecclesiastes 9:11).

To the natural eye, the rule of life seems to be the luck of the draw. As if by a random dealing of the cards, some are born into wealth and influence. Others start their journey with weak bodies, troubled families, and economic slavery. Some are blessed with health and happiness in retirement. Some age in poverty. Some wither in pain. Others die young.

Still, we tell our children that work and wise choices can make up the difference. We tell them that the lazy and unprincipled can expect a hard life. We assure our young that diligence and saving and planning for the future will pay off in the end. But in reflective moments we sense that the rules we teach seem only to work for some of the people, some of the time. To the natural eye, the rest seem governed by the unpredictable, uncontrollable circumstances of life.

Our suspicions, if true, lead to heavier matters. If life is not fair, it seems inevitable that we must also believe that God is not fair, that He doesn't care, or that He has started something that even He cannot do anything about.

We are not the first to doubt God's sufficiency or goodness. The author of Psalm 73 felt his faith crumbling under the weight of unfair circumstances. He was afraid to admit the doubts that gripped him. He was overwhelmed by the injustice of it all, until, in the sanctuary, he saw further than he had ever seen before. It was as if oxygen was breathed into his empty lungs. His faith was renewed and, as if by a miracle, he said, "Whom have I in heaven but You? And there is none upon earth that I desire besides You" (Psalm 73:25). Nothing changed but his perspective.

Then there is the prophet Ezekiel. He also addressed the problem of unfairness, but with less apparent empathy. He quotes the Lord as saying to His chosen people, "You say, 'The way of the Lord is not fair.' Hear now, O house of Israel, is it not My way which is fair, and your ways which are not fair?" (Ezekiel 18:25, 29).

What kind of comfort is this? How could we be unfair to Him when we are so weak and He is so full of options?

A contemporary of Abraham named Job pressed our argument for us. In all of the suffering endured by him and his wife, Job wrestled with heaven over the inequalities of life. And when God had finished speaking, Job was left speechless and comforted (Job 41–42).

What God did not do was give Job the answer of Psalm 73. The Lord did not remind Job that He would use eternity to comfort those who had trusted Him. God didn't even blame

Job's forefathers for leaving him the family inheritance of a fallen world. Nor did the Lord blame Satan for sponsoring all the terrible things that had happened to Job, his wife, and his children.

Instead, God took Job to the forest. He took him to the ocean. To the mountains. To the hazy brightness of a midnight sky. To the flashing violence of a thunderstorm. To the shadow of His presence in nature. To the one who uses the blackness of night to give birth to the morning.

With only a few words, the Lord of creation showed Job the work of His hand. It was as if the Lord of the heavens gave Job flowers and said, "If I could make a flower, or a horse, or the stars . . . do you think I could make a mistake with you?"

Trust Him? That is exactly what we don't want to do. Wait? We don't want to wait. We don't want to listen when He says that unfairness is not His problem, but ours. How could we possibly be unfair with Him?

Father, please do for us what we can't do for ourselves. Lift our focus from our losses to what You have given. Open our eyes to the difference You have made. Let us see that what You do now and will do forever is infinitely greater than anything You have withheld.

March 2004

WHAT TRUST LOOKS LIKE

WHAT DOES TRUST LOOK like when we can't explain our trouble, or see beyond it?

Listening to others as they try to show faith in crisis can be confusing. Some say they are "believing God" for a job, restored health, a reconciled marriage, or the return of a prodigal. Others say reliance on Him means accepting that His ways are not necessarily our ways.

In the waiting room of prayer and helplessness, I've concluded that questions about what it means to trust God can be almost as troubling as the problem itself. I've also discovered that it is for those struggles that the wisdom of the Bible has been given to us.

Don't be too hard on yourself. The most godly men and women of the past were deeply disturbed by the crises of their lives. King David wouldn't eat or be comforted as he pleaded with God for the life of his dying child (2 Samuel 12:16–17). Even though David was a man after God's own heart, the songs and groans of his life reflect recurring fear and despair (Psalm 6:1–7). Job's experience was similar. In the dark nights of his loss, his first expressions of trust turned to bitter anguish (Job 3:1–26). Then there was childless Hannah. Her prayers for a baby were so deep and emotional that her priest accused her of being drunk (1 Samuel 1:13–15). Even the apostle Paul had "great sorrow and continual grief" for unsaved family and friends (Romans 9:2). Together they show us that trust can cry, and groan, and even doubt.

Expect to be misunderstood by others. In times of profound loss and concern, even our best friends will try to make sense of what has happened to us. They may forget that people do not suffer in proportion to their wrongs. Some pay quickly for their mistakes. Others do not. Some suffer for being foolish while others are punished for being wise (Psalm 73:1–14).

Such irony complicated the ancient tragedy of Job. When his friends heard him express bitterness and despair, they wrongly assumed that he was suffering for a secret sin (Job 4:1–9). Although they came to his side to divide his pain, they ended up multiplying it (Job 16:2).

Don't be afraid to be honest with God. An elderly Abraham laughed at the absurdity of God's promise to make him the father of many nations. Jacob wrestled with his Lord over the uncertainty of what lay ahead. David openly expressed his despair and helplessness in circumstances beyond his control. Job accused God of being unfair.

When heaven seemed to be ignoring them, they said so. When they thought they had an argument, they expressed it. They learned to trust God in the dark valleys of their doubts.

Take one step at a time. Sometimes it helps to break the journey down into small steps. Jesus encouraged us not to worry about tomorrow since today has enough of its own problems (Matthew 6:34). In the weakness of turbulent and unsteady emotions we may need to settle for short steps, the wisdom of the moment (James 1:6), and the present reassurance of the one who says, "I will never leave you nor forsake you" (Hebrews 13:5).

Don't be self-destructive. In times of disappointment or distress we need to avoid quick fixes that are harmful or self-destructive. None of us can afford addictions that kill the pain for the moment but complicate our problems in the long run. While there is a time for sedatives and painkillers (Proverbs 31:6–7), they can be abused at great risk to ourselves and others (Proverbs 31:4–5; 20:1). We also need to ask God to help us avoid taking out our anxiety, anger, or despair on those around us. Lashing out can be its own kind of addiction.

Don't underestimate God. One of the great truths of the Bible is that when we are helpless, God is not. A wise person has said, "Of this I am sure: There is a God. And it's not me." If God doesn't answer our prayers in the time and manner that we've asked, it's because He can see what we cannot.

Joseph learned to trust God after being sold into slavery by his older brothers. When he was reunited with them later in life, he was able to say, "As for you, you meant evil against me; but God meant it for good" (Genesis 50:20).

Ask but don't demand. In desperate circumstances we are apt to think we know what we need from God. Like a small child who cannot be consoled, we are inclined to beg Him for what we want, when we want it. In those moments God understands our weakness and fear. Yet He is also the One who uses the depth of the Grand Canyon, the power of Niagara, or the wonder of the night sky to calm us in His presence (Job 38–41). Christian philosopher Francis Schaeffer observes, "When I am in the presence of God, it seems profoundly unbecoming to demand anything" (see Job 42).

Doubt yourself. Job finally got to the place of doubting himself more than he doubted God. After being reminded of the eternal power and infinite genius of the God of creation, he fell to his knees. From a heart that was both broken and relieved, Job said, "I know that You can do everything, and that no purpose of Yours can be withheld from You. You asked, 'Who is this who hides counsel without knowledge?' Therefore I have uttered what I did not understand, things too wonderful for me, which I did not know. I have heard of You by the hearing of the ear, but now my eye sees You" (Job 42:2–3, 5).

Father in heaven, we want to trust You. But sometimes we get so confused. Please forgive us for wanting answers so that we don't have to trust You. Thank You for being so patient with us. Please help us to have the same patience with You, as we wait to see that Your plans and timing are better than our own.

October 2003

WHAT'S A SOFT ANSWER?

I ADMIRE THE PERSON who can use humor, thoughtfulness, or a self-deprecating comment to defuse the tension of an angry moment. Maybe that's why I've become so intrigued with the proverb that says, "A soft answer turns away wrath, but a harsh word stirs up anger" (Proverbs 15:1). I'm convinced that there is more here than a reminder not to yell at one another.

The Neighborhood of This Proverb

The previous proverb reminds us that anger isn't always wrong. Solomon provided needed balance when he said, "The king's favor is toward a wise servant, but his wrath is against him who causes shame" (Proverbs 14:35).

I have a good friend who occasionally reminds me that sometimes I am so committed to avoiding anger that I don't get angry even when it is called for. At its best, angry emotions show that we care enough to be upset when someone or something we value is in danger. This is like the anger of the king who became emotional when one of his servants acted without regard for the needs of others (Proverbs 14:35).

Wisdom, however, keeps this emotion on a short leash. Solomon's "rule of the soft answer" helps us avoid the danger of unnecessary anger.

Anger is like a guard dog. It can help us protect ourselves, our property, or someone we care about. But anger can also be our own junkyard dog. Regardless of whether we call him "Nero," "Porkchop," or "Sunrise," he will act on his own instincts. Without training, fencing, or a short leash, he will bite a friend as quickly as he will attack a thief.

The Motive Behind This Proverb

So what restraint does wisdom give us? Is Proverbs 15:1 just encouraging us to lower our voices to avoid waking the sleeping dog? No, the wisdom described here isn't just about volume. What makes a response gentle is our motive, not our volume. A soft answer is motivated by love.

A voice raised in love is less threatening than a thought whispered in contempt. A loud "Yes, I'm upset. I'm sorry. Forgive me. But I happen to care about you!" is much more calming than a softly spoken "You're nothing but a worthless version of your father (or mother)."

"What I do with my time is none of your business" is a harsh answer even when it's said softly through smiling lips. On the other hand, "What can I say? What I said was thoughtless and mean. You didn't need to hear that from me!" is likely to be "soft" even if expressed with loud regret.

Proverbs 15:1 isn't about loud responses. It's warning us about harsh responses that, even when whispered, awaken anger because they're spoken as a threat. "Soft" words, though, tend to defuse anger, regardless of their volume, because they're an offer of safety.

WHAT WORKS

TREND WATCHERS TELL us that a growing number of Americans are more likely to ask, "Does religion work?" than "Is it true?"

In the past, spiritual seekers asked, "Is there a God and, if so, how can I know Him?" Today, many are more apt to ask, "How can I use spirituality to overcome my addictions, fix a broken relationship, or learn to feel good about myself?"

Are we trying to answer questions people aren't asking?

It's hard for people to care whether there's an afterlife if they're trying to survive an unhappy marriage, long-term unemployment, or over-extended debt. It's a bit like trying to tell people how to find the best restaurant in Washington, DC, when they are only looking for fast food in Pittsburgh.

So how do we get the attention of people who don't even believe in religious truth? Do we start by showing them that Christ can help them find "fast food in Pittsburgh" (i.e., immediate practical help for addictions, finances, or relationships)? Can we assume that if they find Christ helpful in the urgent and material matters of life, they might be willing to think about their spiritual need of Him?

Does Christ help us find what we are looking for?

This question needs to be answered carefully. We know that during Jesus' days on earth, He often responded to people's physical needs as a means of leading them to His Father. His down-to-earth way of bringing people to heaven shows us that meeting people at their point of need is one of God's ways of drawing them to Himself. It is just as true, though, that our Lord was unpredictable. He didn't always give people the answers or results they were looking for.

What if we don't get the help we asked for?

We often hear people give God credit for saving their home, health, or business. But there are other stories out there. Many haven't turned out so well. Or what about those who called out to God and discovered that He was willing to help, but not in the way they had hoped?

What if doing the right thing makes matters worse?

Ironically, doing the right thing often makes matters worse. Whistle-blowers who call attention to corporate crime can pay dearly for their courage. Hard-working employees get mistreated by slacking co-workers who don't want to look bad by comparison. Health workers contract the infectious diseases of their patients. Job of the Old Testament suffered for being good (Job 1). Even Jesus Himself reminded us that those who follow Him might see things get worse before getting better. He showed how costly it could be to follow Him when He said, "Do not think that I came to bring peace on earth. I did not come to bring peace but a sword. For I have come to 'set a man against his father, a daughter against her mother, and a daughter-in-law against her mother-in-law'; and 'a man's enemies will be those of his own household'" (Matthew 10:34–36; 2 Timothy 3:12).

What good is a faith that creates more problems?

One of the most troubling side-effects of following Christ is that our faith in Him might separate us from those we love the most. Take, for instance, a husband who regrets that he has ignored his family while making a god out of his work. He turns to Christ for forgiveness and determines to spend the rest of his life showing his wife and children that he's not the man he used to be. It's now up to the wife and each of his children to make their own call. They might like their new husband and father. Or they might resent him for bringing religion and God into their lives. If it is the latter, the recently converted man might find himself disillusioned with a faith that didn't work the way he thought it would.

What works as far as God is concerned?

We might like to believe that if the Lord answered all of our prayers, we would be more useful to Him. The Bible shows us, though, that God sees our needs differently than we do. He's pleased when we trust Him in the middle of our disappointments.

I'm slowly learning that our ability to help others depends largely on what we have learned in the tough times of our lives. People are more likely to see the power of God working in our weakness than in our strength. The apostle Paul discovered this in the middle of his own struggle. He pleaded with God to remove some unidentified problem from his life, but he learned in the process that experiencing God's strength in his weakness is what he really needed (2 Corinthians 12:7–10).

This inner experience strengthened Paul at a level that he had not expected. But even though it "worked for him," he wasn't merely relying on his experience. His deeper confidence was in the historic resurrection of Christ from the dead. Paul was so convinced that our experience must rest in the truth that he wrote, "If Christ is not risen, then our preaching is empty and your faith is also empty. If in this life only we have hope in Christ, we are of all men the most pitiable" (1 Corinthians 15:14, 19).

When it comes to having a hope and confidence in the middle of our disappointment, nothing does more to keep our heads clear and our hearts calm than to know the truth of who Christ is and what He has done for us. What the Bible shows us is that it is actually more relevant to ask, "Is it true?" than "Does it work?" In time, what is true about God, ourselves, and our future will be far more important to us than "what worked for a while."

Father in heaven, we have tried so often to use You to get the results we long for. In the process we get it all backwards. Please help us to use the results we long for as an opportunity to know You.

September 2003

Beliefs and the Bible

WHAT WE BELIEVE

Do those who don't share our views on God, morality, and public policy enjoy being around us? Or has the tension of moral politics come between us?

If so, here's a question. Is it possible to remain faithful to our own beliefs while fighting for the right of others to disagree with us?

My guess is that most of us would vote to protect a person's right to be a Buddhist, Muslim, or atheist American. Yet, who would deny that voting to protect a person's right to reject Christ is as serious as the public policy issues that are dividing us?

Is it possible that some of us have lost track of what we really believe? In an attempt to clarify our own beliefs, let's see how far we can go together in the following statement of faith:

> While admitting we have no way of understanding where God came from, or why He would exist without beginning or end, we believe we see in and around us evidence of a cause

- ❖ powerful enough to have created the cosmos.
- ❖ personal enough to be the source of human personality.
- ❖ timeless enough to explain the age marks of the universe.

While seeing that life is marked not only by design, but also by chaos, we believe we must come to terms with our sense that

- ❖ something has gone wrong with the world.
- ❖ life is unfair.
- ❖ our mortality stalks us.

While agreeing that the Bible leaves many questions unanswered, we believe the most published book in the world

- ❖ tells a story that resonates with life as we know it.
- ❖ explains our past.
- ❖ gives us hope for tomorrow.

We believe the two testaments of the Bible point forward and backward to One who

- ❖ came at the time calculated by Daniel the prophet.
- ❖ was born in the place predicted by the prophet Micah.
- ❖ died in the manner anticipated by Isaiah and Zechariah.

We believe this long-anticipated Messiah and miracle worker fulfilled the holidays of Israel and bought our rescue by His

- ❖ execution on the Jewish feast of Passover.
- ❖ burial on the Jewish feast of Unleavened Bread.
- ❖ resurrection on the Jewish feast of First Fruits.

While acknowledging that the small nation into which He was born has been a longstanding focus of international conflict, we believe the Messiah of Israel will one day bring peace to the world when He

- ❖ returns in power.
- ❖ turns weapons of war into tools of agriculture.
- ❖ laments the loss of those who refused to accept His offer of mercy.

While believing that Christ will change the world at some unannounced time in the future, we believe He wants to change our lives now as we

- ❖ discover how much He has done for us.
- ❖ invite Him to reign in the kingdom of our hearts.
- ❖ reflect by His Spirit the attitudes of Christ.

While Christ warned His followers to expect rejection, we believe it is important to remember that our Lord was loved by sinners and hated by

- ❖ religious conservatives who defended law at the expense of grace.
- ❖ liberals who defended grace at the expense of truth.

❖ nationalists who wanted political power rather than a spiritual mission.

While acknowledging that followers of Christ are to have a special love for one another, we believe we are also distinguished by

❖ loving our enemies.
❖ blessing those who curse us.
❖ praying for and doing good to those who hate us.

While acknowledging that it is not up to us to control others or to impose our beliefs upon them, we believe it is our mission to

❖ make the life-changing wisdom of the Bible understandable and accessible to all.
❖ help people all over the world have the chance to discover a personal relationship with Christ, grow to be more like Him, and become actively involved in His mission of rescue.

Father in heaven, please forgive us for leaving others with the impression that we think we are better than they are, or that we would like to impose our values on them, or that we want them to live by our faith rather than by their own better judgment. Please help us to make it clear that our calling is to love and inform, not to condemn or control.

June 2006

TRANSLATIONS

SOME GODLY FRIENDS BELIEVE that to have an inerrant Bible, we need more than perfect original manuscripts. They insist that divine preservation must extend to every word of our Bibles. They say that if we allow for any error of transmission or translation, the Scriptures cease to be trustworthy.

Their logic suggests that if we allow for any uncertainty, all certainty is lost. A flawed text produces a flawed authority; a flawed authority produces a flawed faith; a flawed faith produces a flawed salvation; a flawed salvation gives false hope; and false hope is no hope at all.

This kind of thinking sounds compelling. But it is misleading. The one-version-only argument is offset by the principle of inspired repetition. By repetition, the Author of the Bible has protected us from the dangers of a miscopied text or an inadequate translation.

The Spirit of inspiration did not limit Himself to one statement about salvation by faith, the distinction between law and grace, the mission of the church, or the danger of a real lake of fire. He did not limit Himself to one pronouncement about misdirected sexual behavior, the misuse of alcohol, or the importance of prayer. Sacred Scripture repeats its doctrines over and over again through historical narrative, law, poetry, prophecy, parables, and letters.

The sixty-six books of the Bible reflect a wonderfully orchestrated symphony of testimony. As the Bible itself says, "God, who at various times and in various ways spoke in time past to the fathers by the prophets, has in these last days spoken to us by His Son, whom He has appointed heir of all things, through whom also He made the worlds" (Hebrews 1:1–2).

Even at the moment of most holy revelation, God committed the words and actions of His Son to multiple pens. He did not give us Matthew only. We might wish He had. Matthew only would have been simpler. Matthew only would have eliminated difficult problems of historical correlation. But Matthew only was not God's plan.

Instead, He also entrusted the record of His Son to the inerrant writings of Mark, Luke, and John. Then He entrusted His inspired story to the letters of Paul, James, Peter, Jude, and John—not always to provide new information, but to provide a wonderful, jewel-like, multi-faceted revelation of inspired Scripture.

God's Word is wonderful in repetition. It is rich in perspectives. It is deep in complementing parallels that combine their voices to give us the whole counsel of God. It is because of, rather than in spite of, multiple prophets, multiple apostles, multiple translations, and multiple interpreters that we can say with great confidence that we have in our hands the absolutely reliable Word of God. It is because the Bible was spread throughout the world in many thousands of copies that scholars can assure us that only a small percentage (i.e., 3 percent) of the original autographs is in question (none of which jeopardize a major doctrine).

But what about congregational reading? The existence of many versions and paraphrases has created problems for public reading. A church must choose one version to read. In addition, copyrighted versions raise questions about profit motives in a lucrative Bible publishing industry. We need to keep that in mind while also remembering that if the translation is reliable, the "workman is worthy of his wages."

I'm convinced that our biggest problem today is not new translations, or people making a profit off our purchase of the old ones. Our biggest problem is that too many of us are not reading, meditating, memorizing, studying, underlining, believing, trusting, loving, obeying, quoting, sharing, or honoring the Word of God in any translation.

Father, please give us wisdom to honor Your Word. Renew in us the spirit of Psalm 119. Teach us to love You and one another through Your Word more than we ever have before.

April 1996

A MANIFESTO

MANIFESTOS DECLARE revolutionary ideas. The Communist Manifesto of 1848 called for the redistribution of wealth. Martin Luther's Ninety-five Theses in 1517 affirmed salvation by faith alone, and the thirteen colonies' Declaration of Independence in 1776 made a case for citizens' right of revolt.

The most revolutionary declaration of all, however, was the first-century preamble to Jesus' Sermon on the Mount. With fewer words than Lincoln's Gettysburg Address, or Martin Luther King's "I Have a Dream," Jesus of Nazareth turned common values inside out and upside down. With ideas that were as countercultural as thoughts could be, He gave us reason to declare:

WHEREAS the wisest and best man the world has ever known changed history with the point of His words rather than by the edge of a sword, and,

WHEREAS He declined to accept political power, even when it was within His grasp, and,

WHEREAS He taught us to live by the way He died,

BE IT RESOLVED that we will seek to change our own world by the spirit and attitudes we have found in Him.

TO THAT END we confess that our Lord gave us a new way of seeing ourselves and others when He looked at the crowds of hurting people who were following Him and said:

1. Blessed are the poor in spirit, for theirs is the kingdom of heaven.

In the presence of One who healed withered legs and blind eyes, we discovered that our troubles had done us a favor. Our material losses and moral failures had brought us to the only One who could help us. Because we could not help ourselves, we followed Him long enough to hear the words,

2. Blessed are those who mourn, for they shall be comforted.

When our hearts broke under the weight of our own wrongs, this Teacher's ideas made sense. With His help we saw that our problems were rooted not in bad leaders, laws, or circumstances, but in ourselves. Only when we saw our need for forgiveness did we find the comfort we were looking for. Only when we were assured of a better future than we had ever dreamed possible could we see why our King would say,

3. Blessed are the meek, for they shall inherit the earth.

In the presence of One who walked on water, calmed a storm, and spoke peace to the most troubled hearts, we found that being submissive to Him gave us inner strength and courage. In declaring our surrender to Him, we saw that the earth on which we knelt was not ours to conquer but His to entrust. In the assurance of His promise we were ready to hear Him say,

4. Blessed are those who hunger and thirst for righteousness, for they shall be filled.

As we learned new ways of relating to others, we found a peace that replaced our thirst for conflict. As we hungered for His attitudes, we realized that His life began to show up in us. As we responded to others with the patience and love we found in Him, we found a freedom of spirit that soared on the words,

5. Blessed are the merciful, for they shall obtain mercy.

From our Teacher's example we learned that honor is found not by passing judgment on others, but by showing mercy to those already condemned by their own actions. By offering a kindness that was needed but not deserved, we began to breathe the air of heaven. With a river of mercy flowing through our lives we experienced the cleansing promised in the words,

6. Blessed are the pure in heart, for they shall see God.

In new motives we found a purity of heart that allowed us to see more of God than we had ever seen before. As we reached out to others with the grace that had been shown to us, we began to see God Himself working in us and through us. As we watched how He loved people we had once considered untouchable, we began to understand why He would say,

7. Blessed are the peacemakers, for they shall be called the sons of God.

In the cause of peace we found a purpose that reflected the heart and ways of our Father. As we began to see others as people for whom Christ died, we saw how important it was to avoid any alignments or associations that would distract from our mission. Yet because we knew others would misunderstand us as they misunderstood Him, we took courage in the words,

8. Blessed are those who are persecuted for righteousness' sake, for theirs is the kingdom of heaven. Blessed are you when they revile you and persecute you, and say all kinds of evil against you falsely for my sake. Rejoice and be exceedingly glad, for great is your reward in heaven, for so they persecuted the prophets who were before you.

In the promise of eventual reward we were reminded that there is a price to be paid for being faithful to our King. Yet if we had to be resented, we wanted to be resented for the mission He had entrusted to us. While there are many worthy moral and political causes, we knew that, in the end, there would be only one battle that mattered.

WITH THIS CONFIDENCE AND CONVICTION OF MIND, we therefore hold this principle to be self-evident: That what is best for us and for our neighbors does not begin with a change of circumstances, but with a change of heart.

AND, THEREFORE WE RESOLVE, with the help of our God, to make the attitudes of our King the manner in which we seek to relate not only to our friends, but to our enemies as well—for the honor of our King, and for the good of all, for whom He died.

November 2004

PERSONAL BIBLE READING

HOW IMPORTANT IS PERSONAL Bible reading? This question has been eating away at me for several reasons.

1. Most people didn't own Bibles until recently. For most of church history, followers of Christ relied on the *public* reading and teaching of Scripture. Personal copies of the Bible didn't become common until well after the invention of the printing press in the fifteenth century.

2. Personal interpretation of the Bible can be misleading. Although much of Scripture is self-explanatory, the apostle Peter acknowledged that difficult passages could be misused to our own harm (2 Peter 3:16).

3. Knowing what the Bible says doesn't always make us better. Most of us have to admit that on occasion we have used the Bible the way a drunk uses a lamppost—for support rather than light.

At times I've wondered what to do with such facts. While I'm still thinking about them, I find it helpful to remember the following:

Jesus Lived by the Book

Whether introducing Himself as Messiah, teaching His disciples, reasoning with religious leaders, or confronting His adversary, Jesus referred to, quoted, and applied Moses and the prophets. His insightful use of Scripture during forty days of temptation in the wilderness gives us an example of how important the Word of God was to Him. Three times Jesus used the phrase "It is written" in response to three devilish propositions.

Admittedly, Jesus' use of the Scriptures doesn't answer all of my questions about personal Bible reading. In fact, the more I think about how thoughtful and insightful He was in applying the Scriptures, the more I recognize that I have little hope of being able to follow His example. His ability to browse through Moses and find just the right words for a difficult test of character has the opposite effect on me. I could never be as good as He was in speaking truth to the powers of darkness. I can no more use Scripture the way He did than I can walk on water or control the weather.

With this admission of inability, however, I'm nudged by another thought: Jesus couldn't even do what He did. If that sounds irreverent, it's not. On one occasion Jesus said to His disciples, "I can of Myself do nothing. As I hear, I judge; and My judgment is righteous, because I do not seek My own will but the will of the Father who sent Me" (John 5:30).

Even though Jesus was "God with us," He didn't do anything on His own. When the devil tried to provoke Him into an independent display of His power by making a rock into bread or by jumping from a high place, the Son of God refused to do so (Luke 4:1–13). As the apostle Paul later explained, when Jesus left heaven to be born into the human family, He voluntarily laid aside the use of His divine power (Philippians 2:5–11).

Jesus Relied on the Spirit

As Matthew reminds us, even when Jesus did not have His disciples at His side, He was not alone. Neither did He have to rely on the prompting of His own thoughts when reflecting on Scripture that He had previously read, thought about, and memorized. As He began three years of public life and ministry, He saw the Spirit of God coming upon Him (Matthew 3:16). Soon after that He was led by the Spirit into the wilderness to be tempted by the devil (4:1). This repeated emphasis on the Spirit's presence with Jesus is not accidental.

We don't have to study, understand, or apply the words of the Bible on our own either. As we carefully read and think about the intent and timeless principles of Scripture, and as we look for what the events and people of the Bible tell us about God and about ourselves, we can be sure that somewhere within our thoughts the Spirit of God is at work teaching, leading, correcting, and shaping our hearts. Even if we can't separate our thoughts from the mysterious way the Spirit of God is working in us, we can depend on Him as we try in every situation to orient ourselves by the compass of what God has said.

There Are Many Ways to Center Our Lives in the Scriptures and Prayer

Before anyone had versions, paraphrases, and designer editions of the Bible, people who were thirsty for God found ways to reflect day and night on what He has said (Psalms 1; 119). For many generations, people learned Scripture by word of mouth, by repetition, and by memories not dulled by today's information overload. Fathers and mothers told and retold the stories of the betrayal of Joseph, the miracles of the Exodus, the anger of Moses, the courage of Esther, and the scandals of Samson.

Now, as in the past, the life-changing songs and wisdom of the Bible can renew our minds and shape our attitudes. In every imaginable circumstance, the words, thoughts, and stories of the Bible can be used by the Spirit of God to relieve our fears, subdue our anger, and deepen our resolve.

So let's end where we began. How important is personal Bible reading? The answer lies in another question: How necessary is it to meditate on what God has told us about Himself and about us?

Depending on our circumstances, spending a lot of time in the Bible today may not be possible, necessary, or even advisable. But thinking throughout the day about what is important to God is critical to our spiritual well-being. Without telling us how to do it, King David described as "blessed" the person who meditates day and night about the words and ways of God (Psalm 1).

Father in Heaven, on our own we get lost in thoughts, in opinion polls, and in beliefs about You that are not true. Please help us to find ways to think throughout this day about what You have said and shown us through Your Word. By the presence of Your Spirit we need Your Word to be a lamp to our feet and a light to our way.

May 2007

NEW BELIEVERS

WHY DO NEW BELIEVERS often show more evidence of spiritual life than those who've been around for a while? Sometimes, when I look at my own heart, and then at those just coming into the family, it seems as if those who've known the Lord for the shortest period of time love Him the most.

While I've seen many examples of Christians who have grown more loving and committed with time, the opposite pattern occurs enough to warrant some thought. See if what I've been thinking makes sense.

The Honeymoon Effect

The enthusiasm of new believers seems to parallel the honeymoon phase of marriage. What starts in the soft light and warmth of a new day soon cools in the deepening dusk of mutual disappointment.

Because of the tendency to go backward rather than forward, our Lord had to ask one of the best of all first-century churches for a renewal of "first love" that had been left behind (Revelation 2:4).

The Impact of Contrast

A new look gets more attention than a familiar one. Just as we notice changes of appearance in a friend or co-worker, it is natural to be impressed by the "new look" of a babe in Christ.

The apostle Paul reminded Christians in Thessalonica that, as new believers, they'd become examples to all when they "turned to God from idols to serve the living and true God" (1 Thessalonians 1:7–9).

The Casualties of War

Another reason for new believers' enthusiasm may be that they've not yet been neutralized or sidelined by the enemy. Bad blood, burnout, bitterness, moral scandal, disappointment, distraction, and disillusionment are common human reactions. They also play into the hands of the "serpent stalker" who is trying to make sure that we're all distracted by good times or the bitterness of bad times.

I'm convinced, however, that it would be a mistake for those of us who've been in Christ for a while to blame our loss of momentum and affection on the natural course of time, or the supernatural influence of our "accuser." Other factors also explain why new believers are often our best examples. For many reasons, seasoned Christians lose enthusiasm for the Word of God, for prayer, for spreading the gospel, or helping others. And here's what I think happens.

The Effect of "Club Rules"

As new converts, we're defined not by the rules we've kept but by the beliefs we've embraced. We experience spiritual birth not by mastering a list of laws but by believing that God has come into our world and into our lives to help us. But these beliefs are soon subject to competing interests. As new believers are welcomed by older Christians, the spiritually young are faced with a new set of expectations (see the discussions in Romans 14 and Galatians 3). New converts must learn not only the ropes of biblical essentials, but the cultural preferences of the group they have joined. The possibilities are endless.

Understanding church culture and "club rules" is important. Good manners, social courtesies, and shared values are the way we look out for one another. But stated or unstated rules of preference eventually take on a life of their own. Subtly but surely, the number of expected meetings, dress codes, political and economic alignments, and doctrinal fine points are subject to group control.

Quite unintentionally, living by "club rules" becomes more important than living by right beliefs. It's understandable. Groups can't control hearts but can apply social pressure to unacceptable behavior. At the same time, converts eventually discover that it's pretty easy to live by "club rules" of appropriate dress, conduct, and attendance at required meetings. It's much more difficult to trust God in the inevitable tests and strains of relationships.

But there's a pitfall in this shift from beliefs to external appearances. Even in essentials, the life of Christ isn't found from rule to rule, but from faith to faith (Romans 1:17). It's from one act of believing to the next that an admitted sinner discovers what it means to be declared legally righteous, mercifully forgiven, warmly adopted, and spiritually empowered by the Father in heaven.

Beliefs are so important because affection and enthusiasm for God are formed in belief before they are formed in action (Galatians 3:5). Even though the existence of faith can be challenged if there are no actions (James 2:20), it is also true that acting without a heart of faith is merely going through the motions.

When we become less likely to act in a Christlike way, when our enthusiasm and love for the Lord cool, when we go through the motions without the gratitude of first love, the problem isn't that the honeymoon is over. The problem isn't just that we no longer have a new look. Nor that we've succumbed to our enemy, or to mindless conformity to club rules. The real problem is that we've stopped thinking and believing in our hearts like real followers of Christ.

Father, You know how often I've lost my first love for You. You know how often I've tried to find acceptance in the expectations of the important people in my life. You know how inclined I am to hide behind poorly kept external rules and conformity.

If it were not for what Your Son believed and sacrificed in my behalf, I'd have no hope. Please renew in us the beliefs that deepen the faith of the aged and bring enthusiasm to the young.

July 1998

SHADOWS OF DOUBT

Dear Mel,

I've been thinking about the spiritual doubts you were struggling with the last time we talked. I didn't say much at the time because I didn't know what to say.

Now that I've had a chance to collect my thoughts, I want you to know that I respect you for admitting that you've been dogged by questions about the fairness of life and the goodness of God.

I also want you to know that I don't blame you for saying you don't like being around religious people like me. There was a day when I would have resented your comment. But I've come to see that there is a lot of truth in your opinion of us. People like me do have a tendency to imply that every problem can be solved with the medicine of morality. And all too often we spend more time defending our beliefs than in caring for others.

I also believe you are right in recognizing the unfairness of life. We don't all suffer in proportion to our wrongs. Neither do we all prosper in proportion to the good we do. Some abuse their bodies without consequence. Others try to take care of themselves and get sick.

How could a good God let this happen? Where is His sense of justice? How can we walk through a children's hospital or a psychiatric facility and still believe in the goodness of God? How can we see the terrors of war, and famine, and flooding and still believe that a good and powerful God is in control? There isn't one of us who would let such terrible things happen if we had the power to stop them.

Mel, you don't need me to tell you that I don't have answers for these questions. What I do want to say is that I care that you've had more than your share of problems and losses lately.

I also wanted to write because I've been reading through some old papers and letters I think you'd be interested in. Inside one of the oldest papers, I found the account of a man whose story reminds me of yours. He was hurting and couldn't understand why. His religious friends all argued that he was suffering because of some sin he was hiding. As it turned out— *they* were wrong.

As I worked my way through these papers, I compared that man's story with the experiences and thoughts of a person whose name I know you'd recognize. He's a person religious people love to quote, even though religious people were His worst enemies. This person didn't follow the party line to explain suffering. He didn't believe that all people suffer in proportion to their own wrongs. He said it was a mistake to assume that people who die in accidents or live with physical suffering are paying either for their own sins or the sins of their parents.

Mel, what makes this person so interesting is the people who were attracted to Him. Hurting and rejected people were drawn to Him. Religious people resented Him. But I think you would have liked Him. I know He would have loved you.

What am I implying? Would He have called down a sign from the sky to convince you that there is a God in the heavens? Would He have taken the time to answer all of your questions and objections to faith? I'm not sure He would have done either. Even though He was known to do miracles and answer tough questions, He didn't do miracles or answer questions on command.

His method was more personal. He seemed to see the hearts of everyone He met. Those who were proud looked into His eyes and saw nothing but themselves. Those who were broken looked into the same eyes and saw the heart of God. Those who were doubting to avoid the truth learned to hate Him. Those who were doubting to know the truth ended up on their knees before a God who cared for them.

Mel, I don't want to imply that this Person has answered all my questions. He hasn't. But He has shown me that He deserves to be trusted with what I don't know. He helps me believe in God even though I can't see the gates of heaven. He reminds me that ideas and actions have consequences even when the results are not yet evident. He helps me believe that the best is yet to come, without needing to know when.

I haven't always been so sure of my faith. I've often been where you are. I have doubted the fairness of life, the goodness of God, and the credibility of religious answers. Even at the present I feel, in most respects, that I can't rely on my own ability to see clearly. What I have come to believe is that I can depend on His eyes. I believe I can trust Him to see for me when He looks at the pain of this world—then calmly lifts His eyes and prays to His Father in heaven.

At this point, I don't know if you can relate to what I see in His eyes. That's why I'm hoping you will spend some time with Him yourself. Get to know the way He thinks. Watch the way He relates to different kinds of people. Listen to Him as He prays. Look at Him when He cries. Then I think you will see what I see in His eyes.

Thanks, Mel, for reading this. If you're interested, I'd love to talk more. I'm confident that this Person is someone you can believe in. As you get to know Him, I'm sure that you could even come to love and trust Him as much as I do.

Sincerely,
Mart

P.S. I'm sending copies of this letter to some other friends too. I hope you won't mind, but I think some of them might be wrestling with the same questions and doubts that you are.

May 2000

TWO THIEVES

CRUCIFIXION WAS TORTURE. Leather straps or spikes were used to hang a condemned man on a pole. Like a helpless animal tangled in a barbed wire fence, the victim could survive for days in excruciating pain. Death usually came by suffocation when, hanging by his hands, the victim lost the strength to draw another breath.

Three Men on Three Trees

In the spring of 33 AD, the crucifixion of three men, outside the city walls of Jerusalem, changed the course of world history. Roman executioners hammered nails through the wrists and ankles of three men and left them to die. The event itself was common in the ancient Roman-dominated world. And yet, 2,000 years later, the world still talks about those three deaths.

I found an explanation of the significance of those deaths written on the flyleaf of my grandfather's Bible. In words I have found memorable, my grandfather M. R. De Haan wrote, "One man died with guilt in him and on him. A second man died with guilt in him but not on him. The third died with guilt on him but not in him." Since finding that quote, I've held on to it as a profoundly simple description of some differences we all need to understand.

One Died with Sin in Him and on Him

He was the first of two thieves executed that day. By the law of the land he was given the punishment he deserved. By a judge wearing the authority of the Roman Caesar, he was sentenced and condemned.

The first thief seems to have died an angry man. He was probably angry with himself for getting caught. He was probably angry with the judge who sentenced him. He was probably angry with all those who had let him down along the way. He seems to have been especially angry with the man named Jesus who hung innocently at his side.

The first thief wasn't alone in his contempt for Jesus. Others shared his feelings. It was easy to be furious with someone who claimed to be the light and hope of the world—then hung like a common criminal, not even saving Himself from death.

Angry with Jesus for being unable to help Himself or anyone else (Luke 23:39), the first thief died with his own sin in him and on him.

One Died with Sin in Him but Not on Him

There was a second thief executed that day. At first he joined the others who ridiculed and insulted Jesus. For a while he too mocked Jesus with the challenge to save Himself and them if He really was the promised Messiah (Matthew 27:37–44).

As the darkness closed in, however, the second thief had a change of heart. Turning to the first thief, he said, "'Don't you fear God, since you are under the same sentence? We are punished justly, for we are getting what our deeds deserve. But this man has done nothing wrong.' Then he said, 'Jesus, remember me when you come into your kingdom.' Jesus answered him, 'I tell you the truth, today you will be with me in paradise'" (Luke 23:39–43 NIV).

That may be one of the ten most important conversations ever recorded. These few words show what the rest of the New Testament declares. Forgiveness of sins and eternal life is given to anyone who believes in Jesus. Nothing more. Nothing less. Faith alone in Christ alone determines our eternal destiny (John 3:16–18; Acts 16:31; Romans 4:5; Ephesians 2:8–9; Titus 3:5).

The second thief had no time to clean up his life. He had no time to do anything but to believe in Jesus. In the process, he gave all of us a picture of what it takes to come into the eternal family of God.

In response to the simplest expression of faith, Jesus assured him of forgiveness. The second thief died with sin in him but not on him. The Judge of the heavens lifted the guilt from the second thief's shoulders, placing it instead on Jesus, our sin-bearer.

One Died with Sin on Him but Not in Him

Jesus shouldered the guilt of the world that day. He died with the weight of the world's sin on Him but not the slightest wrong in Him.

Three days later He rose from the dead to show that His death, tragic as it was, was not a mistake. With a nail-scarred, resurrected body Jesus gave hundreds of His disciples all the evidence they needed to believe that He had taken their place in death. The judgment of God had fallen on Him instead of on us.

What I also find amazing is that this is our story. We were there. We were there because God was there in our place, bearing our sins. We were also there because all of us will respond either as the first thief or as the second.

The words don't make the difference; the faith does. If you don't have that faith, but want it, ask God to give it to you. You won't be the first to cry out, "Lord, I believe; help my unbelief!" (Mark 9:24).

Father in heaven, thank You for helping us to see that this is Your story. In the suffering of Your Son, we see Your suffering and Your love for us. In His death, we see Your payment for our wrongs, and Your offer of forgiveness. In His resurrection, we see Your assurance that You are completely pleased with the price He paid for us.

And Father, thank You also for helping us to see that this is our story. In the first thief we see our first inclination to hate You, to reject Your love, and to let our anger keep us from You and others. Thank You for softening our hearts so that we can also see ourselves in the second thief, who came to his senses before it was too late.

May 2000

RELIGIOUS CONSERVATIVES

WHY ARE THE VILLAINS IN the greatest story ever told a group of religious conservatives?

The question is personal. I am a religious and biblical conservative. I believe in the importance of the family and am convinced that our children need to learn the dangers of Darwin, abortion, and same-sex marriage. Theologically, I'm a fundamentalist. I believe in moral absolutes, the authority of Scripture, and the uniqueness of Christ. What I can't shake, however, is the thought that the most dangerous group of people in the New Testament were not atheists, secularists, religious liberals, or advocates of sexual freedom. The most dangerous group in the New Testament were:

Politically active
Religiously conservative
Protectors of a spiritual heritage

One thing that made this group dangerous is that they looked so good when compared to others. Pagan neighbors used male and female prostitution as part of their religion. Roman patriots worshiped Caesar and named him among their gods. Occupying forces were brutal in demanding unfair taxes at the point of a sword. The current king of the Jewish people was a madman who used slave labor to build enormous fortresses for his own protection but killed anyone, even wives and children, who got in his way. Yet none of these were as dangerous as the Pharisees because none of the others were as zealous for the Law and rule of God (Matthew 23:15). No one else spoke as loudly on behalf of Moses while calling for the death of Christ.

A defining moment. Although they had to fight dirty to get rid of Him, the religious right got their way. They swung the vote of the mob and pushed the buttons of government. A few hours later, the pride of Israel had their man. The teacher they hated was hung on a tree like a predator on a fence post.

The would-be messiah from the back roads of Galilee was no longer a problem—until rumors of His reappearance began spreading like wildfire. First a group of women reported that the teacher's tombstone had been moved and that His grave was empty. One woman reported seeing Him alive. Then others said they too had seen Him. Groups of men and women who had been cowering in the shadows came out with a story they were willing to die for.

In the hours that followed, some of Jesus' enemies admitted they had been wrong. Others were enraged at the spreading opinion that the moral elite of Israel had just killed their own Messiah.

How could it happen? How did the most conservative group in Israel become the villains of the Bible? What were these men thinking? How could they allow themselves to be cast in this role? How could people who had been waiting hundreds of years for a Messiah end up killing the very One they had been waiting for?

Because "it takes one to know one," I think I can understand some of what was happening. Religious conservatives knew they were right. They knew the dangers of pagan influence. They understood what happens on a slippery slope of compromise. What they didn't see was that their strength had become their weakness. Their good had become their god. Their light had become their blindness.

Could it happen again in me? As I read the New Testament, I see myself not only in the disciples who loved Jesus but also in the religious conservatives who hated Him.

I have been a friend of Israel at the expense of Arab people for whom Christ died. Blinded by my desire to be among those who bless the "chosen people," I have forgotten that God chose one nation for the sake of all. I have also ignored the example of the prophets. From Moses to the Son of God, they remind us that a friend does not flatter (Amos 3:1–8; 7:14–17). Neither does a real friend of Israel encourage her to find her security in military strength or international allies.

I have made gods out of biblical accuracy, doctrinal soundness, and moral absolutes. To my deep regret I have often been more concerned about being right than in showing the compassion of Christ to those who know how wrong they've been (Matthew 12:9–14).

I have honored men to the loss of women Christ loves (John 12:1–7). On too many occasions I have underestimated the contributions of women and disrespected my own wife with foolish, self-centered talk about male headship.

I have aligned with political conservatives to the detriment of my own principles. While pointing out the sins of the left, I have ignored sins of the right. I have forgotten that political alignments are temporary while people on both sides of the aisle are eternal (Romans 1:13–16).

I have deferred to the rich at the expense of the poor. I've forgotten that even the best arguments for capitalism do not justify oppression, mistreatment, and disregard for those in need (James 2:1–9).

I have deferred to self-appointed protectors of American culture at the expense of internationals. While much can be said for the spirituality of America's founders, I have too often aligned with those who use historical, Judeo-Christian roots to support political efforts that alienate others from the gospel.

Seeing my mistakes renews in me a desire to know not only the truth of Christ but also His attitude. On that road I haven't traveled very far. But of this I am sure: If my son or daughter were to convert to Judaism or Islam, to join another political party, to identify with the unchurched or unreligious, or even to renounce their citizenship and salute the flag of North Korea, Syria, or Cuba, I would be building bridges rather than burning them.

Father, please help us to avoid the mistakes of those who defended Your Word, Your people, and Your laws while unintentionally and unknowingly hating Your Son—and those for whom He died.

July 2003

MIRACLES

WHY DO I BELIEVE IN miracles? Because I believe in God! I believe in the King who turned sticks into snakes before the demon-empowered magicians of Pharaoh's court. I believe in a God who can supernaturally open national borders, blind eyes, and closed minds. I don't doubt His ability to suspend or override natural law.

I doubt instead any theological system that uses opinion or dispensational boundaries to limit the intervention of heaven. The Lord of history has not stopped giving gifts. He has not forgotten how to enable His people to speak in real languages they have not learned. Nor has He forgotten how to bring order out of chaos, light out of darkness, or life out of death. God is the same yesterday, today, and forever.

I believe in a God who can enable His servants to walk on water, heal the sick, and raise the dead. I believe in a Lord who can enable paralyzed, withered legs to stand, walk, and run. I believe in a God who will use time and eternity to heal all of His people from all of their diseases, neuroses, and sins. I believe in a God who can use apostolic gifts in regions of the world where the gospel message needs authentication. I believe in the real presence of angels and demons, and in spiritual warfare.

What don't I believe? I don't believe in those who promise healing, material prosperity, and the salvation of lost loved ones in exchange for "faith shown by a check" made out to their ministry. I don't believe in miracle-promising fundraisers who make pre-Reformation excesses look honest by comparison.

Why don't I believe in these claims and promises? One reason is that it is not clear their best results are any different than the experiences of non-Christian religions. Spontaneous, unexplainable recoveries are not restricted to Christian crusades or networks. Miracle healings have long been claimed by Christian Science, New Agers, and pagan cults.

I believe in a God who can use all of us in spite of ourselves. I am thankful for the good He does, sovereignly and mercifully, through those who trade false promises of miracles for dollars. But how can we not be deeply concerned about the dishonesty of an industry that has grown on the back of consumer fraud and false prophecy? The Old Testament is clear about the danger hanging over those who use God's name to make predictions or claims that are not true.

Do I discount all reports of those who have experienced relief from arthritis, high blood pressure, or stomach ulcers? No. Do I discount all claims of visions and voices in the night? No. Do I discount the experiences of godly people who have seen God do amazing things in their lives? No. I discount the claims of brothers and sisters who do not deliver what they are promising, while building crusades and media conglomerates on the basis of false advertising and wrong doctrine.

How can I dismiss the claims of so many of God's people? How do I dare risk quenching the Spirit and closing my eyes to the work of God in these last days? I can do so because it is not true that God wants all of His people to experience material prosperity and physical health in this life. It is not true that God is handing out promises of healing, prosperity, or salvation of loved ones in exchange for generous love gifts to money-raisers. Nor is it true that physical healing for this life is part of the atonement.

But aren't waves of first-century miracles sweeping over Canada, the United States, and the British Isles? Not to my knowledge. In spite of rumors and claims to the contrary, I don't know of anyone who has been wheeled into a healing meeting with shriveled legs and walked out whole. Wheelchair-bound quadriplegics brought by loving parents and friends leave the same way they came. What is different is that now they have the additional burden of wondering what could have happened if they would have had more faith.

While people with invisible afflictions walk out of a meeting claiming their healing as a necessary requirement for receiving it, those with observable maladies leave only with the reality of a condition that has not been changed, and that cannot be denied.

Father, forgive us for believing more and less than the truth. Please give us the ability to believe without being gullible, to hope without presumption, to love without lies. Help us to trust You for whatever You choose to give or withhold. Help us to trust You when You say, "Do not quench the Spirit. Do not despise prophecies. Test all things; hold fast what is good. Abstain from every form of evil" (1 Thessalonians 5:19–22).

June 1997

FREEDOM TO CHOOSE

COULD IT BE TRUE THAT God determines who will go to heaven, but leaves us with the impression that the choice is ours?

Some students of the Bible are convinced that the doctrines of total depravity, foreknowledge, election, predestination, and sovereign grace are essential to an understanding of the grace of God. They believe that the alternative to these doctrines gives too much credit to human choice, human intelligence, and human character. Others say that free will and choice are foundational to the heartfelt response God wants from us—that without freedom of choice we end up being puppets rather than persons.

So who is right? Let's see if some definitions are helpful.

Total depravity is the teaching that every part of our being has been damaged by sin. In our natural state, none of us will look for the kind of God who has made us for Himself (Romans 3:10–12). So unless God intervenes, we will continue wandering from Him in spiritual darkness.

Foreknowledge and election mean that even before creation God foreknew and chose those who would be saved (Romans 8:29–31). Some understand this to mean that in His foreknowledge God chose those He knew would choose Him. Others are convinced that people like those described in Romans 3:10–12 will not choose God unless He first chooses them and enables them to believe.

Predestination means that God has predetermined that those who believe in His Son will eventually be conformed to the likeness of Christ (Romans 8:29–31). Some think this is a kind of action that overrides human will and choice. Others see it as the action that works with our will to assure that the salvation we desire will be fully realized.

Sovereign grace is a term used to emphasize that salvation begins and ends with God alone, and that because of our inclination to wander away from Him this rescue is an expression of God's undeserved kindness to us.

Now back to our questions. Have we been so damaged by sin that we will only choose God when He intervenes in our behalf? Do we move toward God only when He moves us?

Just about the time I am thinking freedom to choose is only an illusion, I remember the Old Testament story of Job. In a conversation that took place in heaven, God asked Satan to consider one man who stood out from all the rest of mankind. Satan's response was that Job was better than other men because God had bribed him to behave well. According to the adversary, God was giving Job protection and wealth in exchange for Job's faithfulness.

Satan's argument was significant. It focused on Job's choices and motives, not on the accusation that God had sovereignly caused Job to be better than others. Satan acknowledged that

Job chose to serve God, but said that he did so from self-serving motives. Satan's comments combine with the Lord's to show that Job was an issue of conversation because of Job's choices. Nothing in the story leaves God open to the charge that Job was merely a puppet-servant who did what God programmed him to do.

Where does this leave us? I think it leaves us once again with a sense of the mystery and wonder of God. It also leaves us with an opportunity to find our bearings by orienting ourselves to what we know, rather than to what we don't know. By going back to truths we've already accepted, we can conclude:

1. A right view of foreknowledge and election will deepen our appreciation for the goodness of God. If our thoughts about election and predestination cause us to doubt that God is inexpressibly wonderful, we can safely conclude it is our understanding of what we don't know that is flawed (Psalm 34:8).

2. A right understanding of God's sovereignty will ignite a passion to reach the lost. The men and women of the New Testament set a pace for us. They risked their lives to give others a chance to hear and believe what Christ has done for us. They believed what God wants us to believe, and they acted in a way God wants us to act. If our understanding of free will and sovereignty kills our concern for others, then it is our thoughts that are flawed.

3. A right view of God's sovereign grace will promote humility rather than pride. Any truth rightly understood leads us to a God who in turn causes us to see ourselves and one another in His shadow (Deuteronomy 29:29).

4. A right view of election and predestination will prompt Christlike love for fellow believers. Together these truths show how much God has done for His family. The example of

His eternal love is a strong reason for us to care for one another as He has cared for us.

5. A right view of free will gives honor to God. Nothing is more basic than that God deserves honor for being what we could never be, and for doing for us what we could never do for ourselves. Our salvation in time and eternity begins and ends with Him. We are the ones who have messed up. He is the one who has come to our rescue. His choices are what we need to honor.

Again, I don't know how to sort all of this out. But I'm confident of this: The Bible wants us to take our own choices seriously, even if only to keep saying, *Yes, Lord, I do invite You to live Your life through me. Please do for me what I cannot do for myself. I do want to be under the influence and control of Your Spirit.*

July 1999

SHOULD WE GO KOSHER?

DO FOLLOWERS OF CHRIST have a moral obligation to keep the Ten Commandments? Even though this seems like an easy question, I've struggled with the answer.

Why Is This a Hard Question?

The question of our relationship to the law of Moses is thorny for a number of reasons. People who believe in the Bible have disagreed about whether all of the Ten Commandments are eternal moral principles. The issue comes up because the ten laws are part of a covenant God made with the nation of Israel. By contrast, those who believe in Christ have entered into a new covenant of grace.

New Testament letters to the Hebrews and to the Galatians warn followers of Christ not to put themselves back under the law. The apostle Paul reasoned that we are neither forgiven nor made mature by trying to keep the laws of Moses. Yet the New Testament writers never stop promoting the moral principles that are at the heart of the Ten Commandments.

The question of the Ten Commandments is also complicated by whether we honor Saturday, Sunday, or some other day as our day of rest and worship. Some wrongly assume that Sunday has become our Sabbath. Yet Sunday did not become a day of rest until the fourth century when the emperor Constantine declared it so.

Another complicating factor is that Jesus said He didn't come to do away with the law but to fulfill it. Instead of denying the law, He raised it to new heights by teaching His followers to honor the spirit of the law by loving one another, their neighbors, and even their enemies.

According to Jesus, the law was more far-reaching than other religious leaders thought it was. In His Sermon on the Mount He showed that the Ten Commandments are rooted in issues of the heart. He taught that we violate God's law against killing when we hate—and when we harbor lustful thoughts, we commit adultery in our hearts. Later, the apostle Paul wrote that when we covet, we commit idolatry (Colossians 3:5).

Should We Go Kosher?

For these reasons and more, a growing number of believers are asking us to rethink our relationship to the law given by God at Sinai. They are saying that if we follow Christ as He wants us to follow Him, we will keep the seventh-day rest. We will eat kosher. We will live a Torah-observant life—not to earn forgiveness but to receive wisdom.

I would not want to discourage anyone from eating kosher, from keeping a seventh-day rest, or from observing as much as possible the Jewish calendar of feasts and holidays. There is insight to be found in the laws and calendar God gave to Israel. That is, as long as no one thinks we have a moral obligation to keep forms of the law that were designed by God to be shadows of the Messiah (Colossians 2:17). There is wisdom in the law as long as we do not think that worshiping God in old covenant law is better than worshiping Him in New Testament grace.

The Covenant of Moses Had a Limited Purpose

Most of the covenant of Moses regulated temple worship, ritual sacrifice, the duties of priests, or a kind of civil or criminal law that could be practiced in Israel only until the destruction of the temple.

Of the 613 laws God gave to Moses, some protected historic land boundaries. Others prohibited the sale of property to those outside of the family. One law required a brother to marry the widow of his deceased brother. Other laws called for adult male attendance at national holidays three times a year in Jerusalem.

The most important reason for the new covenant, however, is not that the law of Moses had a limited purpose. The most important reason for the new covenant is that Israel consistently broke, and was broken by, the terms of the earlier covenant. As any nation of imperfect people would have done, Israel broke covenant with her God and fell under the curse and condemnation of the commandments.

The New Covenant Is a Better Solution

The new covenant is international in scope (Ephesians 3:4–6). It is a better covenant for people living both inside and outside the national boundaries of Israel. The new covenant offers a better assurance of being accepted by God, a better sacrifice (Hebrews 7:19, 22; 8:6; 9:12–14), and a more complete understanding of law (Galatians 5:13–14). The new covenant writes the laws of God on our heart (Hebrews 10:16).

So what parts of the laws of Moses apply to us? For our health and protection we need to honor those timeless principles of

Moses that also appear in the pages of the new covenant. In New Testament terms they are a part of what is called "The Perfect Law of Liberty" (James 1:25; 2:12). Faithful members of the new covenant honor these moral principles in their heart. They honor them while depending on the work of Christ and His Spirit to do for them what they could never do for themselves.

There Is Irony Here

Our new covenant experience is a foretaste of what will happen to Israel in the last days. The prophet Jeremiah predicted a day when the Lord God would make a new covenant with the nation of Israel. In that day He promised to give a remnant of Israel His Spirit, to write His laws on their hearts, and to forgive their sins (Jeremiah 31:31–34).

The old covenant of Moses enabled Israel to be a distinct people and a witness to all the nations of the world. Now, for a season, the tables have been turned. Internationals who believe in Christ have become messengers to the chosen nation of Israel.

From heaven's point of view, good laws are of little benefit if they are on the books without being in our hearts. Good laws condemn us if we have no way of being forgiven when we fail to keep them.

So do we have a moral responsibility to keep the Ten Commandments? Yes, if we mean the moral principles that are at the heart of the law. Yes, if we acknowledge our new covenant dependence on Christ's payment for the laws we've broken. Yes, if in our own effort we are relying on the Spirit and the grace of Christ.

The new covenant writes the law on our hearts.

November 2000

THE STORY FACTOR

SOME PEOPLE SPEND A lifetime trying to understand the Bible. Others reduce it to a few basic principles.

In *Walk the Line*, a film portrayal of country singer Johnny Cash, a conversation between two young brothers suggests another approach. During a reflective moment, just before a tragic accident changes their lives, the boys are lying on their beds. Jack, his older brother, is reading his Bible when Johnny asks, "How is it that you read and remember all those stories in there?" Jack responds, "J. R., I wanna be a preacher someday, so I've got to know the Bible front and back. You can't help nobody if you don't know the right story to tell them."

Jack's desire to know a story for every occasion might seem boyishly naïve. Or it might sound like one side of a current debate. A growing number of scholars and church leaders believe that the unfolding drama of the Bible is at the heart of its life-changing power. Others, however, are convinced that focusing on stories, instead of teaching doctrine, has become a trend that is watering down the authority of the Bible.

As in so many controversies, there is truth on both sides of the issue. The Bible is more than romance, mystery, and adventure. Between its covers we also find the laws of Moses, the songs of David, and the letters of Paul. Yet, even the laws, songs, and letters of the Bible have a story behind them.

The story factor of the Bible raises important issues. As the plot of the Bible unfolds, even some things as basic as the Ten Commandments are not given directly to us. The laws written in stone are part of the unfolding drama of God's relationship with His chosen people. In a similar way, the parables of Jesus and the letters of Paul are also part of what God was doing with a group of first-century people. How, then, can they be God's Word to us?

How does God speak through a story?

How can any part of the Bible be for us, if all of it tells the story of God's relationship with ancient tribes, disciples, or churches? How can we say this is God's Word to us when we are looking over someone else's shoulder?

Some would answer these questions by saying that the value of narrative lies in its ability to mean something different to whoever hears it. Others would say that while it's clear that the stories of the Bible are designed to engage both our imaginations and our hearts, they are also written to help us resist our tendency to make the Scriptures say whatever we want them to say. By weaving together people, events, and ideas, the plot and subplots of the Bible provide a context for understanding the author's intent. Every story tells us something about God and something about ourselves that we will either act on or ignore.

Consider, for instance, the story Jesus told His disciples about a wealthy man's desire for a return on his investments. According to Jesus, the man divided some of his assets among three workers before leaving on a journey. While he was gone, two of the men invested the money entrusted to them and had a profit waiting for the owner when he returned. The third, however, hid his money "under the mattress" to protect it. The employer was not pleased. He rejected his employee's excuse by saying, in effect, "You knew that I expect a return on my investment" (Matthew 25:14–30).

In this parable, the employer didn't tell his workers how to put his money to work for him in his absence. What is clear, however, is that they all knew him well enough to make their own choices as to what they should do while waiting for his return.

What about us? Does the most-published book in the world tell us enough about God and ourselves to enable us to serve Him as we wait for His promised return? Or are we already rehearsing our own excuses?

Imagine saying to Christ upon His return, "Lord, it's so good to see you. I've been so confused. I kept waiting for You to tell me what You wanted me to do. You were so silent. All You left was a book full of someone else's stories. They were all about people living in a different time and place. I had my own problems. I needed to know what You wanted me to do."

Can you imagine the Lord saying, "What more did you need to know? You knew what I was like from the stories of My relationship with Adam and Eve, Abraham and Sarah, and Moses and Miriam. You heard how I responded to the prayers and wrongs of David and Solomon. By My involvement in their deeply flawed and troubled lives, you saw that I could walk with you on paths of your own choosing rather than Mine."

Suppose the Lord continues, "You're right. The Bible is the story about My relationship with people who lived a long time before you. Every one of those stories told you something about Me and something about yourself. That's as much as I wanted you to know. I didn't give you the Bible to answer all your questions. Then you wouldn't have had to trust Me. I was more interested in telling you stories that would help you answer *My* questions. Once you knew what I was like and how far I would go to bring people of all nations to Me, would you want to do what you could to help? Would you be thankful for what I had done for you? Would you care that I love you? Would you trust Me to guide and enable you?"

Father in heaven, forgive us for hiding behind what You have not told us. Help us to be like young Jack, who wanted to know Your book from front to back—the stories that tell us what we need to know about You and about ourselves—for the sake of those for whom Your Son died.

May 2006

MISBELIEFS

DOES WHAT WE BELIEVE MATTER? Growing opinion suggests that what we believe is likely to have little to do with how we live.

In his "Index of Leading Spiritual Indicators," researcher George Barna shows that on the surface Americans remain some of the most religious people in the world: 93 percent of adults say they believe in the existence of God; 89 percent agree that "there is a God who watches over you and answers your prayers"; 88 percent say they believe Jesus was a real person; 85 percent say they believe Jesus was crucified, died, rose from the dead, and is spiritually alive today; and 58 percent maintain that the Bible is totally accurate in all of its teachings.

Behavior, however, tells a different story. When it comes to things such as dishonesty, charitable giving, cheating, prayerlessness, Bible reading, divorce, sexual activity outside of marriage, pornography, abortion, and physical and sexual abuse, polls show a widening gap between what we say we believe and what we are actually doing.

The problem is not that what we believe is unimportant. The problem is that over time we can develop a widening gap between our formal beliefs (which express the tenets of our faith) and our functional beliefs (which shape what we do at any given moment). This occurs in dimensions of our lives which, for the sake of illustration, we might call the "upper" and "lower" stories of belief.

Upper Story

This represents our formal beliefs. It is the language of the faith given to us by God. In creed form it sounds like, "I believe in God the Father, in Jesus Christ His Son, and in the Holy Spirit. I believe in life after death, in heaven, hell, and the coming judgment. I believe in salvation by faith in Christ, apart from works, and solely on the basis of God's grace."

Stairway

This is the twilight zone of unexamined thoughts, attitudes, beliefs, and competing values. It is the place where we mindlessly adopt the language and logic of self-deception. Here we say things like, "I think it's important to pray, but I also need to be getting things done." It is here we say, "I think it's important to be willing to stand alone on moral issues, but I also need friends."

Lower Story

This is the main floor, the foundation of functional belief, the origin of the language of self-rule. After walking down the stairs of self-deception, we confess to a religion based on our own autonomy. It is here we think in phrases like these: "I don't have time to think about it. This is no big deal. I have an excuse. I know what I have to do. No one knows my needs better than I do. I can do it myself. I need to have my way. I have a right to be happy. I have a right to be free of pain. I have a right to expect other people to come through for me. If I don't protect myself no one else will. Other people are doing a lot worse. My problems are someone else's fault. I can afford to take my chances. I've gone too far to turn back now. I can expect God to help me solve my problems on my terms. I can avoid the consequences of my choices. I can't afford to admit when I'm wrong. When I do wrong, I'm not hurting anyone but myself. I don't owe anyone anything."

Soon after conversion or soon after a spiritual crisis, those "upper story" beliefs are likely to weigh heavily on us. In the warmth of our new awareness, which has come upon us like the dawn of a new day, we are apt to remember the coolness and darkness of the night from which we've come.

But soon, without strong effort and opportunities to renew our mind, the language and beliefs of the flesh begin to come in like a rising tide, displacing the influence of Christ-centered thoughts. Before long, we are once again a strange mixture of people who say we believe in God and yet we believe we can trust Him on our own terms.

This subtle but predictable process is one of many reasons we need to recover a passion for the Word of God. We need the Word of God in our thoughts and in our hearts so that what we believe will line up with our confidence in God, our ever-present Provider.

The Bible makes it absolutely clear that I am considered blameless by God, and that I grow spiritually in my awareness of Him not as result of what I do but as a result of believing what I have heard God say (Galatians 3:1–3). The righteousness of God is revealed from faith to faith (Romans 1). I am changed by opening up the beliefs of my "lower story" to the cleansing and renewing words and Spirit of God.

Father in heaven, please renew our confidence in the faith You have given us. Help us to know in our hearts that what we believe does matter. Enable us to know deep within ourselves that our relationship with You, and with everyone You bring into our lives, is rooted in whether we are thinking about what You have said to us, and whether we believe by Your grace in allowing Your Son to live through us.

October 1997

THE ROAD TO REALISM

SOMEONE HAS NOTED THAT, "Optimists think the glass is half full. Pessimists think it's half empty. Realists know that if they stay around long enough they're going to have to wash the glass."

In art, realists paint life with blemishes, wrinkles, and scars. Idealists paint a subject as they imagine it could or should be.

On the road of life, both are important. Ideals give us direction. Realism gives us traction.

Both, however, have their downside. Realism can cost us our dreams. Idealism can consume our days in a futile search for the perfect marriage, employment, or happiness.

Idealism and realism also show up in matters of faith. Some think of God as an obsessive, demanding parent who cannot be pleased. Others think of Him as an indulgent grandparent who is so endearing and compassionate that there is no reason to fear Him.

What do we think? Is God a realist or an idealist? It's a question that brings us to a busy intersection of ideas. If we aren't careful, we will run into traffic coming at us from both the right hand and the left.

The danger of these crossroads, however, is worth the risk of getting past them. While looking both ways and proceeding with caution, many have found a God who is good enough to inspire us with His ideals, merciful enough to accept us as we are, and too loving to leave us there. This, it seems, is the story of the Bible.

In a perfect world, we would live forever. That's how the drama of the Bible begins and ends. Within the opening chapters, however, our first parents lose their innocence and immortality. Their first son kills his younger brother and from then on a succession of good days and bad days take turns raising hopes and ruining them.

The realism of a beautiful world stalked by conflict and death, however, is not what makes the Bible an all-time bestseller. What makes this Book so compelling is that its rugged realism offers strength for the journey with a vision for a better world at the end of the road. Someday, according to the prophet Isaiah, weapons of war will be recycled into tools of agriculture (2:4), and even a defenseless lamb will eat safely at the side of a wolf (65:25). In the end, those who make peace with God now will find perfect peace forever.

Yet the idealism of the Bible is not just about the future. Both Testaments also call us to love God with all our heart and to love our neighbor as ourselves. Both emphasize not only the moral rule of "love," but also the virtues of "joy, peace, long-suffering, kindness, goodness, faithfulness, gentleness, [and] self-control" (Galatians 5:22–23).

No society passes laws against such ideals. Yet no one consistently lives up to them either. So how do we come to terms with our imperfection?

In a real world of human weakness, first-century Judaism had an answer for moral limitation. Some rabbis taught that a person who observed any important commandment, such as forsaking idolatry, was equal to the person who kept the whole law.

Interestingly, a New Testament author by the name of James takes a different approach. He writes, "Whoever shall keep the whole law, and yet stumble in *one point*, he is guilty of all" (James 2:10, emphasis added).

At first look, the rabbis who focus on the law we keep rather than on the one we break seem more realistic. James, on the other hand, seems to be setting a trap of perfectionism. Break one law, he says, and you break them all.

On second look, though, will a "Keep one, and you keep them all" approach allow us to sleep any better? Who of us has kept even one law perfectly? Who has loved our neighbor as ourselves? Who, when the heart of idolatry is understood, has forsaken all false gods? Who has not coveted?

Interestingly, James is not the idealist that 2:10 seems to suggest. When he presses the logic of law, he does so only to get the attention of self-righteous persons who refuse to receive or show mercy (vv.12–13). He writes as a follower of Christ (1:1), and believes that his faith in Christ compels him to pursue neighbor love in the most realistic and down-to-earth ways (1:26–2:8).

The people James has a problem with are those who talk as if they are friends of both idealism and realism—without honoring either.

Dangerous Drivers

The religious leaders who called for Christ's death had the law of God in their minds but not in their hearts. Publicly they were experts in the Law. Privately they created legal loopholes that allowed them to ignore the compliance they required of others.

Publicly they argued the moral ideals and logic of the slippery slope. They made laws around laws, like fences around fences, to keep less thoughtful people from trespassing the boundaries of Moses. Privately they were realistic enough to know that they had to break their own laws to get rid of the rabbi from Nazareth who was making them look like hypocrites.

Merging from the Right and Left

Jesus was kind to people that other religious leaders avoided. He ate and drank with people that other religious leaders wouldn't be caught dead with. He touched lepers, talked respectfully with women, and loved noisy children.

In Jesus, the most inspiring idealism comes together with the most rugged realism. Nowhere do we find a better picture of what it means to be faithful to the highest principles while offering mercy to the most broken people.

When Jesus pressed the logic of moral idealism, He did so in order to lovingly humble self-righteous people (Matthew 5:20–48). When He offered mercy instead of morality, He did so to show that He had come not to condemn but to rescue (John 3:17; 12:47).

Father in heaven, thank You for showing us through Your Son that there is no conflict between the heights of Your ideals and the depths of Your mercy. We will be eternally grateful that You have loved us enough to accept us as we are and loved us too much to leave us where You found us. Please help us to extend both to others as You have given them to us.

March 2007

Life in Christ

AVOIDANCE

THERE'S A FLINCH. A mental dodge. I sense an inner aversion when I read words like, "as He who called you is holy, so be . . ."

Why don't I like the word *holy?* Why does a word which means "separated to God from sin" prompt the same emotional reaction as the thought of going to the doctor for a physical? Would I rather be sick? Am I more comfortable with a little inner dirt than the thought of being clean and healthy? Or do I get edgy around the word *holiness* because I'm not sure what, in practical terms, the Lord is asking me to do?

I honestly believe that if God would tell me in clear, audible, and unmistakable terms what He wants me to do to be holy, I'd want to live that way. I just don't want to wear a white robe and sandals, throw my television and computer in the trash, cancel the newspaper, and then find out I've acted like a Pharisee. I want to be sure that I'm right before letting the idea of "holiness" loose in the house of my life.

I also know that even if God did talk audibly to me, I'd still have a problem. I know about Jonah.

I'm guessing it is by God's design that we haven't been told what holy people wear, how many times a day they pray, or what kind of activities they avoid or commit to. I think most of us have already come to the conclusion that our Father isn't sitting in heaven checking off a "jobs done" list. Instead, He's looking at our hearts.

I could be wrong, but I think He might say, "So, you have questions about what it means to be holy in the twenty-first century? You've looked at the way My holy Son lived. You've listened carefully to what I am constantly saying to you through the Scriptures. But you still aren't sure how what I've said translates into real life. Well, let's go with as much as you do understand."

What if the Lord told us He'd settle for as much holiness as we know how to give Him, and that He'd cover what we didn't know with the blood of His Son?

I'm convinced we make more and less of holiness than we need to. We make too much of what we don't know, and too little of what we do. We allow what we don't know to push us away, while failing to move toward Him with what we are sure about.

Father, our problem is far more than a flinch. We see Jonah in us, and Judas, and Peter, and the Pharisees. Thank You for loving us enough to accept us the way we are, and for loving us too much to leave us that way. Please use our hearts to live Your holy life through us today.

June 1995

SPIRITUAL WARFARE

IN ONE OF THE OLDEST stories of the Bible, the heart of a mere mortal gets caught in the crossfire between a rebel leader and the King of the universe. According to Satan, God has bought the heart of a man named Job by giving him protection in exchange for his loyalty.

In response to the charge of bribery, God allows Satan to test Job with a series of heartbreaking losses. In the wake of Job's suffering, three friends and a bystander deepen his misery by accusing him of hiding a sin that would explain his suffering. In a series of eloquent arguments, and escalating anger, Job and his friends insult and alienate one another until God speaks out of a storm and brings their conflict to an end.

Although God didn't give Job the answers he was looking for, Job's story combines with the rest of Scripture to give us insight into the ancient art of spiritual warfare.

God Builds Hedges of Protection

Job faithfully interceded for his children. His prayers are an indication of his character. Yet even Job was not able to "pray a hedge" of protection around his loved ones. As the prologue shows, the King of heaven is the one who set the boundaries for Job's spiritual enemy (Job 1:9–12). God is the one who, in His own wisdom and goodness, builds fences and takes them down. If we don't make this distinction, we might put more confidence in our prayers than in our Lord.

The Devil Isn't Our Biggest Problem

Job's story is a timeless reminder that even though we have adversaries in high places (Job 1; Ephesians 6:12), we also have the potential of being our own worst enemy. God had Satan on a leash. The rebel couldn't do anything more than God allowed him to do. The real ambush came from within Job and his friends. They were all blindsided by their inclination to rely on their own understanding rather than to trust God for what He alone could see and explain.

Don't Underestimate the Enemy

God didn't ask Job to match wits or muscle with the prince of darkness. He reserved that role for Himself. According to the New Testament, to speak arrogantly against Satan is a mark of false teaching (2 Peter 2:10–12). Even Michael the archangel showed humility and deference to God in his own struggle with the devil. Instead of presuming that he had authority over Satan, Michael did not dare challenge his enemy but said, "The Lord rebuke you" (Jude 8–10).

Adopt a Truth-Based Strategy

When our Lord met demon-possessed people, He often used His authority to send demons running. But when Jesus, Himself, was tempted by the Devil He resisted His enemy by repeatedly quoting the Word of God (Matthew 4:1–11) in response to each of Satan's propositions. The second approach shows up in a classic New Testament passage that likens our spiritual defenses to the gear of a Roman soldier (Ephesians 6:10–18).

1. *The belt of truth* reminds us how important it is to *tell the truth*. Personal integrity is a priority of spiritual conflict. Even when fear of being exposed tempts us to lie, it is far better to come clean than to trip over ourselves in the presence of our enemies. Lies are self-defeating. A commitment to be honest with God, others, and ourselves is foundational to doing spiritual battle.

2. *The breastplate of righteousness* has at least two implications. First, it represents the protective gift of blamelessness our Lord uses to protect those who trust Him. No one can successfully condemn the person justified by Christ (Romans 8:31–34). Second, this critical piece of body armor reminds us to *do the right thing*. Our enemy loves to catch us doing anything that would jeopardize our mission and give him an unguarded path of access into our lives.

3. *Feet covered with the preparation of the gospel of peace* gives us reason to *be ready for action*. We have been called to endure hardness as good soldiers of Jesus Christ (2 Timothy 2:3). Our path will not be easy. We need to be ready to run on the difficult, rocky ground that lies between us and those who need our help to make peace with the One who died for them.

4. *The shield of faith* reminds people under attack how important it is to *trust the Lord* rather than their own natural thoughts and emotions. Missions of rescue are not for the timid. The enemy knows how to frighten us with arrows of fear and doubt. Yet it is safer to trust Christ in the heat of battle than to hide in bomb shelters of our own making.

5. *The helmet of salvation* is described elsewhere as "the hope of salvation" (1 Thessalonians 5:8) and reminds us how important it is to *think future*. Like Job, we may not be able to understand what is behind the present circumstances of our lives. God wants us instead to protect our minds by taking confidence in a salvation that protects us now and waits for us in heaven.

6. *The sword of the Spirit* is the Word of God. In spiritual conflict we need to remember to *count on what God has said* (Deuteronomy 29:29). Our father in heaven intentionally withholds many of the answers our hearts cry out for. He asks us to trust Him for what He alone can see.

7. *The alertness of a soldier* reminds us that "Praying always for one another" is our spiritual guard duty. *Intercession for others* is a way of showing that we know our enemy can be defeated not by our strength, but by the Spirit of God in His time and in His ways.

Father in heaven, we are often confused by the trouble You allow into our lives. Help us to depend on what You alone can see in this present darkness. We want to resist the Evil One who hates You. Please teach us to bow with Your servant Job before the overwhelming truth of Your unlimited, authority, power, and wisdom.

January 2005

THE VALUES OF CHRIST

MEL FISHER HAS BEEN called the world's greatest treasure hunter. His motto "Today Is the Day" came true on July 20, 1985, when his team found the mother lode of their dreams in the tropical waters of the Florida Keys. After years of salvaging shipwrecks of lesser significance, Mel's team discovered stacks of silver bars, chests of silver coins, gold, and jewels on the ocean floor. They also recovered thousands of other artifacts from the *Nuestra Senora de Atocha*, the richest Spanish treasure ship ever lost in the Western Hemisphere.

People like Mel intrigue and inspire us, because we are all fortune hunters at heart. We all spend enough time with our hopes and dreams to understand the principle that "where your treasure is, there your heart will be also" (Matthew 6:21).

What do we consider important?

At the very least, we are all hunting for happiness, significance, and love. Many of us are also doing our best to find a comfortable home, reliable transportation, and good food. Along the way, we value meaningful work, restful weekends, and friendship. We make sacrifices as we look for good health, physical safety, and financial security.

Such values make us all treasure hunters. All are important, and all seem to have been in mind when the wisest of teachers said to His disciples, "All these things the nations of the world seek after, and your Father knows that you need these things. But seek the kingdom of God, and all these things shall be added to you. Do not fear, little flock, for it is your Father's good pleasure to give you the kingdom" (Luke 12:30–32). According to Jesus, this kingdom was like a "treasure hidden in a field" (Matthew 13:44).

What are the values of Christ?

When Jesus spoke of "the kingdom of God" as the ultimate treasure, He used a term His Jewish countrymen understood. He knew they were looking for the coming of a Messiah and a return to Eden marked by goodwill and world peace. What His countrymen were slow to understand about this coming world order is the value it would place on salvaged wrecks.

Mel Fisher looked for lost treasure. Jesus looked for lost people. Mel Fisher built a museum of salvaged artifacts. Jesus was building a community and kingdom of salvaged lives. Jesus treasured people others despised. He loved His enemies at His own expense. He honored those who admitted their need of others. He held dear those who cared for others. Above all, He valued His Father in heaven, who loves all of us far more than we love one another or even ourselves.

How are our values like the values of Christ?

The importance Jesus put on human need shows that our interests are closer to the heart of God than we might think. Before becoming our Teacher and Savior, Jesus was our Creator

(Colossians 1:16). He is the one who gave us our desire for good food, friendship, and happiness. He built us to look for relational intimacy, personal acceptance, and freedom from worry. As the God who created our capacity to think, He gave us a thirst for knowledge, discovery, and value.

How are the values of Christ different from our own?

Although there are similarities, the treasures our Lord lived and died for differ from our own in several ways.

1. He knew how to be grateful for the gifts of life without worshiping them. We are inclined to make goods into gods, and then into demons that destroy us.
2. He taught us to use the material resources of this world to love people. We are more apt to love things and use people.
3. He taught us to see the joys and pains of this present life as the reflection of a world to come. We sometimes live as if there is no heaven or hell beyond the present.
4. In the pursuit of our dreams we often act as if the treasures of life are beyond ourselves and beyond our ability to find them. Jesus taught us to see that there are treasures of perspective within ourselves that we often overlook.

One of the countless gifts of Christ is a sense of priority and timing. In His Sermon on the Mount, the Teacher from Nazareth puts our values in perspective (Matthew 5:1–10). With a few words of timeless wisdom He shows us how to ultimately find what we are looking for. According to Jesus, the most well-off people in the world are not the materially rich and famous. Those who are to be envied and congratulated are the ones who see their desperate need of God and of one another (Matthew

5:3). The most blessed of all are those who mourn their wrongs to the point of surrendering to God (Matthew 5:4–5). With submissive hearts, they hunger for relationships that give them a chance to show others the mercy they themselves have received (Matthew 5:6–7). With hearts full of love rather than lust, they seek to bring lost people back to God and to one another—even at their own expense (Matthew 5:8–10). These are the attitudes that lead us first to one another and then to the priceless kingdom that has been prepared for us.

We admire Mel Fisher because he and his crew found the sunken treasures of the *Atocha*. We applaud his success. Yet in our more thoughtful moments we remember the One who is really the greatest treasure hunter who ever lived. He looked for the love-filled will of God and found it. He searched for lost people and rescued them. At the expense of His own life, He paid for treasures infinitely greater than material convenience. Then to those who would trust Him, He said: "Blessed are the poor in spirit, for theirs is the kingdom of heaven."

Father in heaven, You have given us so much. The miracle of life is beyond our understanding. The opportunity to know You is a gift beyond comparison. The people around us are priceless. Please forgive us for losing sight of what is most important. Please forgive us for ignoring You, Your will, and the hurting and lost people for whom Your Son died. May today be the day that Your kingdom comes and Your will is done in us, as it is in heaven.

January 2004

OUR IDENTITY IN CHRIST

IDENTITY THEFT IS A PROBLEM most of us didn't think about five years ago. Today it is common to hear the stories of victims who are trying to salvage their name and credit rating after learning that someone has stolen and misused a password, social security number, or charge card.

Knowing the danger of identity fraud will help us think twice before giving personal information that could permit others access to our bank account. Being informed can also deepen our understanding of a spiritual principle that I have often taken for granted. According to the Bible, we are not the only ones who have reason for concern (Romans 2:24). God Himself takes a risk with His identity whenever He allows us to use His name. When we identify ourselves as His children, and when we let it be known that we are followers of Christ, His credit rating gets mingled with our own. Yet by endangering His own reputation, God gives us the greatest of gifts.

The use of His name and credit is at the heart of what the Bible says God does for us. It is not a privilege we would expect or ask for. It's natural to want to take care of ourselves, to solve our own problems, and to be obligated to no one. Yet, from a biblical point of view there are compelling reasons to see our need for access to God's name and credit.

According to the Scriptures . . .

In ourselves, we have problems we cannot solve. That's one reason Jesus taught His disciples to pray, "Forgive us our debts, as we forgive our debtors" (Matthew 6:12). These words remind us that there is something wrong with us. With endless excuses and rationalizations we live for ourselves at the expense of others. God knows this better than we do. Without His forgiveness, we have no ability to get out of the mess we've gotten ourselves into. But . . .

In Christ, we have solutions to our problems (Ephesians 1:3–23). By having access to His name and credit, our spiritual obligations are paid and our legal problems with the law of God are cleared (Ephesians 2:1–10). Fear of rejection, ultimate failure, and death are all solved when God sees us "in Christ." Struggles for personal meaning and value are no longer burdened by our own flawed efforts. In God's eyes, no one is more important, and no one is more secure, than the one He has entrusted with the name of His Son.

One with Him. According to the New Testament, being "in Christ" doesn't depend on our own efforts. We can't do this by ourselves. When we believe in Him, we are placed "into one body" by His Spirit (1 Corinthians 12:12–13). As a result of being joined to Him we become one with Him. His Father becomes our Father, His family our family, and His inheritance our inheritance. "In Christ" we are forgiven, accepted by God, and assured of never-ending life. Because we have become one with Him, we will never again be alone.

One with each other. According to Paul's letter to the Galatians, those who are one with Christ also become one with one another. So the apostle writes, "As many of you as were baptized into Christ have put on Christ. There is neither Jew nor Greek, there is neither slave nor free, there is neither male nor female; for you are all one in Christ Jesus" (Galatians 3:27–28). Race, status, and gender have nothing to do with the value of every person. Those who are in Christ discover that the oneness they have in Him is far more important than their differences.

Remembering Who We Are

Because our identity "in Him" doesn't change what we see in the mirror, we need to work against the inclination to forget our family relationship to Christ. Unless we consistently renew our thoughts, we eventually make the mistake of thinking that our well-being depends on the affirmation of those around us. Visible circumstances incline us to become so obsessed with our physical health or financial independence that we lose our sense of security in Christ. We forget the One who says, "I will never leave you nor forsake you" (Hebrews 13:5).

Protecting His Name

Living in the name and presence of Christ is life's greatest opportunity. It means more than the hope of being forgiven and accepted by God. Our position "in Him" means even more than being able to use the "charge card" of grace in every moment and circumstance of life. Beyond assuring our own well-being, it means we have a family and moral obligation to honor the One who has entrusted His name and credit to us.

The privilege is priceless. It is greater than having access to the world's deepest pockets or bank accounts. If handled well, we have an opportunity to reflect well on the credibility of God (Titus 2:10). If we abuse the privilege, we take God's name in vain—not in profanity, as we usually think of it, but in a way that hurts the reputation of heaven (Romans 2:24).

Because of these opportunities, and with deep concern for the family and credit rating of God, the apostle Paul wrote, "What shall we say then? Shall we continue in sin that grace may abound? Certainly not! How shall we who died to sin live any longer in it? Or do you not know that as many of us as were baptized into Christ Jesus were baptized into His death? Therefore we were buried with Him through baptism into death, that just as Christ was raised from the dead by the glory of the Father, even so we also should walk in newness of life" (Romans 6:1–4).

The message is clear. God doesn't give us the charge card of grace to waste on thoughtless purchases. He gives us the name of His Son, so that at His expense we can buy a whole new way of living and loving.

Father in heaven, we so often fall back into old ways of thinking "in ourselves." Forgive us for falling back on the merits of our own name and accomplishments. Please help us to show by our attitudes and values that we have found life not in ourselves, but in Your Son.

February 2004

MISPLACED TRUST

IF GOD IS GOOD, BUT GOOD isn't God, how do we avoid making some of our worst mistakes with the best things in life?

In an effort to clarify the problem of misplaced trust, what if we said to our hearts: Love God, but don't depend on your love for Him. Seek to know Him, but don't rely on your own understanding. Make it your purpose to serve Him, but don't ever imagine that He's indebted to your service. Make it your objective to please Him, but don't depend on your own efforts to do so.

Listen to your conscience, but don't depend on your own ability to discern right from wrong. Plan your way, but don't presume to know what's ahead.

Seek good relationships, but don't depend on good relationships. Try to find the company of wise people, but don't stake your life on their counsel.

Know the Word of God, but don't make a god of your knowledge. Surround yourself with good teachers, but don't idolize them. Feel sorrow for your sin, but don't count on your sorrow to assure rightness with God.

Count your money and manage it well, but don't suppose that any amount of money can secure safety or satisfaction. Establish budgets to discipline your use of resources, but don't depend on your budgets. Work hard, but don't depend on your work.

Sacrifice for the sake of others, but don't depend on your sacrifice. Be generous, but don't depend on your generosity. Seek to be self-disciplined, but don't rely on your own self-discipline. Seek at all costs to be good, but don't rely on your own goodness or godliness.

Be clever, but don't depend on your cleverness. Seek to be wise, but don't trust your wisdom. Try to understand yourself and others, but don't lean on your own communication skills.

Be kind, but don't rely on your kindness. Love others, but don't be proud of your own love. Give gifts to others, but don't depend on your gifts to accomplish the intent for which you gave them. Work hard to be a peacemaker, but don't make peace into a god. Be faithful to others, but don't rely on your own faithfulness.

Seek to be successful, but don't bank on your own accomplishments. Try to be efficient, but don't rely on your own efficiency. Be careful, but don't depend on your own carefulness. Work to make good decisions, but don't depend on your own decisions. Develop a strategy, but don't count on your strategies. Set goals, but don't depend on your goals. Define clear and measurable objectives, but don't count on your objectives.

Pray, but don't make an idol out of your prayers. Make worship a priority, but don't depend on your worship. Know your spiritual gifts, but don't pin your faith on them.

Entrust yourself to others, but don't depend on others. Follow good leaders, but don't depend on good leaders. Surround yourself with good advisors, but don't rely on your advisors.

Read good books, but don't depend on books. Value friendships, but don't depend on your friends. Be careful about your appearance, but don't rely on good looks. Try to stay healthy, but don't depend on your own efforts to be healthy. Enjoy rest, but don't live for your weekends. Exercise your body, but don't trust your exercise to assure well-being and health. Try to live a long life, but don't count on a long life.

Enjoy good times, but don't depend on good times. Be thankful for today's provisions, but don't lean on these provisions for tomorrow.

Value a good education, but don't worship education. Learn from your mistakes, but don't depend on what you've learned. Use technology, but don't depend on technology. Invest your money wisely, but don't count on your investments.

Try to think clearly, but don't depend on your own thoughts. Try to reason logically, but don't be conceited about your own thoughtfulness. Value your accomplishments, but don't become puffed up over them.

Honor your parents, but don't live for your parents' approval. Love your children, but don't make gods of them. Enjoy your grandchildren. Pray for them. Give them your love and example. But don't tie your hopes and dreams to their choices.

Father, help us to hear You when You urge the wise not to trust in their wisdom, nor the strong to depend on their strength. Help us to hear You when You invite us to rely on this and this alone—that we know You, the everlasting God (Jeremiah 9:23–24). Teach us, Father, to trust what You have done for us through the undeserved provisions of Your Spirit, Your Son, and Your grace.

And help us to hear Your servant when he lovingly writes, "The Son of God has come and has given us an understanding, that we may know Him who is true; and we are in Him who is true, in His Son Jesus Christ.

This is the true God and eternal life. Little children, keep yourselves from idols. Amen" (1 John 5:20–21).

April 2005

WHAT GOD SAID TO ME

WHAT IF I TOLD YOU THAT God has been speaking to me about an issue that I haven't been able to put out of my mind?

Because you know me, you don't think I'm claiming to have heard God speak in an audible voice. You assume that I have had an idea that I believe has the signature of God written all over it. So you decide to hear me out.

Listen to What I'm Saying

You hear me say, "I've been praying about what we can do to reach more people with the message of hope and peace, and the Lord has laid on my heart that we've been too cautious. We need to believe God for miracles, take risks of faith, and commit ourselves to outreach projects that, admittedly, are beyond our ability to afford. After asking God for clear direction, He has given me a pretty amazing vision for an idea I want to talk to you about."

As you listen, you try to keep an open mind, but are not able to share my enthusiasm. You think the idea sounds more like presumption than a way to show our faith. But you don't say this to my face, because who are you to tell me that I haven't heard from the Lord?

What Are You to Make of This?

What's happening here? Why am I able to believe God for a miracle but you are not? Is it possible that I have a sensitive ear to the Lord's leading while you are more inclined to depend on human logic? Or am I using "spiritual talk" as a cover for my own ambition?

These are not easy issues to talk about. None of us want our efforts for Christ to be motivated by human agenda. We want our leaders to be prayerful, spiritually sensitive, and responsive to what they believe God wants us to do. The Bible makes it clear that God uses people to speak on His behalf. The apostle Paul advised the Thessalonians, "Do not quench the Spirit. Do not despise prophecies" (1 Thessalonians 5:19–20).

I'm convinced, though, that the possible misuse of spiritual-sounding language and "God talk" gives us reason to think carefully about how we use phrases like these:

"God has been speaking to me . . ."
"I've been praying about this . . ."
"The Lord has laid this on my heart . . ."
"God told me to say . . ."
"I was led to come to you . . ."
"God revealed to me . . ."
"God reminded me of a Scripture . . ."
"God called to my mind . . ."

What Are the Motives?

Sometimes we talk like this to let others hear our desire to be in step with God. On other occasions we use such phrases as a way of writing God's signature under our ideas to make it difficult for others to disagree with us. We sense, even subconsciously, that when people hear us talk about "what God has laid on my heart," they will be less apt to ask questions.

We Can't Afford to Be Gullible or Naïve

After saying, "Do not quench the Spirit. Do not despise prophecies," the apostle Paul went on to say, "Test all things" (1 Thessalonians 5:21). The apostle John also said in his first New Testament letter, "Test the spirits to see whether they are from God" (1 John 4:1 NIV). Both Paul and John reflect a caution that had been expressed earlier by the prophet Ezekiel. In the sixth century before Christ, he quoted God as saying, "Son of man, prophesy against the prophets of Israel who are now prophesying. Say to those who prophesy out of their own imagination: 'Hear the word of the LORD! This is what the Sovereign LORD says: Woe to the foolish prophets who follow their own spirit and have seen nothing!' " (Ezekiel 13:1–3 NIV).

A Subtle Misuse of Quotes

If we casually say, "God said to me" or "The Lord spoke to my heart," we blur the lines between what we *know* God said in His Word and what we think He might have said through our inner awareness.

This erasing of boundaries is an important issue. Even under the inspiration of the Holy Spirit, the apostle Paul was careful to distinguish between the Word of God and his own personal conviction (1 Corinthians 7:10, 12).

At stake is our own discernment and the honor of the Word of God. If in normal conversation we speak as if what God says to us through our inner inclinations is equal to what He has said through Scripture, we are competing, even unintentionally, with the authority of the Bible.

Honoring the Word of God

So the question then becomes, "How *do* we speak for God?" After all, the apostle Peter wrote, "If anyone speaks, he should do it as one speaking the very words of God" (1 Peter 4:11 NIV).

Our answer needs to be rooted in an honest and reverent respect for the difference between our thoughts and God's thoughts. If we are sure that God has said something in Scripture, we need to quote Him accurately and with conviction. If we believe we are thinking in a manner that is consistent with His thoughts, then we need to say, "I think," or "I believe this is a course of action that would please God," or "I believe this direction is consistent with the teachings of Scripture." The key factor is honesty.

The addition of "I think" or "I believe" may seem like a small matter. But the issue is big. It is the issue that God Himself expressed to Ezekiel when He said, "They say, 'The LORD declares,' when the LORD has not sent them; yet they expect their words to be fulfilled. Have you not seen false visions and uttered lying divinations when you say, 'The LORD declares,' though I have not spoken?" (Ezekiel 13:6–7 NIV).

Dear Lord, Help us to be sensitive to Your Spirit. We want to speak in Your behalf. We don't want to misquote You. Please help us to show complete confidence in what You have revealed, while being open to questions about our own judgment and opinions.

THE SOUNDS OF MUSIC

THE SOUND OF WORSHIP has hit a sour note. In many congregations, changing styles of music have become a source of conflict.

Some church members miss the loss of doctrinally rich hymns. On the other side of the aisle is a generation that seems to thrive on new songs, more volume, and repetitive lyrics.

Over the years, I've been on both sides of the fence. Sometimes I've been insensitive to those who are older. At other times I've felt that the music of the young has crossed boundaries of reverence and good taste. At this point, I think I understand less about music than I did thirty years ago.

What I'm sure about, however, is that none of us can afford the high cost of bitter dissension. Regardless of whether we sing praise songs or hymns, accompanied by piano, synthesizer, recorded music, or live orchestra, everyone loses if the reputation of Christ is damaged by church people who become embittered toward one another.

Furthermore, we can't afford to let our differences cause us to lose confidence in God's gift of music. The Scriptures make it clear that God Himself has given us music for a number of important reasons.

The Gift of Music Is a Way of Lifting Heavy Hearts

In a well-known Old Testament story, a shepherd musician named David used the sounds of strings to relieve fitful episodes of depression that sidelined the sitting king of Israel (1 Samuel 16:23). Certainly the biblical account is not saying that music is a cure-all for depression. But David's use of his instrument does show that skillfully presented music can have a powerful, if temporary, effect on the emotions of our heart.

The Gift of Music Is a Way of Teaching One Another

The longest book in the Bible shows the value our God puts on music. The book of Psalms was given to help us express praise and worship with the sounds of music. According to the New Testament, though, the Psalms are also part of a musical strategy to teach the Word of God. The apostle Paul wrote, "Let the word of Christ dwell in you richly in all wisdom, teaching and admonishing one another in psalms and hymns and spiritual songs, singing with grace in your hearts to the Lord" (Colossians 3:16).

The Gift of Music Is a Way of Expressing a Spirit-filled Heart

The same apostle also called for the use of music as he taught fellow believers how to live a life filled with the Spirit of Christ. In his letter to the Ephesians he wrote, "Do not be unwise, but understand what the will of the Lord is. And do not be drunk with wine, in which is dissipation; but be filled with the Spirit, speaking to one another in psalms and hymns and spiritual songs, singing and making melody in your heart to the Lord, giving thanks always for all things to God the Father in the name of our Lord Jesus Christ, submitting to one another in the fear of God" (Ephesians 5:17–21).

The Gift of Music Is a Way of Showing Our Love for One Another

Because all Scripture throbs with the principle of love, we can be sure that Spirit-filled expressions of music and Spirit-filled responses to music will be marked by sensitivity and concern for others.

I've been impressed over the past couple of decades as I've watched members of my parents' generation endure the music of a younger set. I've watched mature men and women who would have preferred singing more familiar hymns graciously tolerate the songs of the young. I knew it was their spiritual maturity and deep love for their children and grandchildren that made them willing to put up with music and volume that grated on their nerves. I could see that nothing was more important to these parents and grandparents than that their children learn to know and love Christ with all their hearts.

I wish at times that younger people could be as sensitive to their parents and grandparents. Certainly there are times and occasions to adjust volumes and modify style out of respect for those who have brought us to this point. Expectation of maturity, however, should not be wasted on the young. It is when "we are old," according to the apostle Paul, that we put away childish thinking and learn the self-sacrificing meaning of love (1 Corinthians 13).

The Gift of Music Is a Way of Expressing Grateful Hearts

Several times the Psalms call for a "new song" (for example, Psalm 40:3). The reason is clear. New mercies call for new expressions of praise. Does this mean God doesn't want us to sing old songs? No. Old songs, and even old psalms, can be wonderful ways of renewing our appreciation of our God. But the heart attitude is the issue. Our Lord wants songs in our hearts in an ongoing way. The point is not only what happens in the order of service of our public meetings, but in the silent melodies that run through our hearts in the course of a week. The music He calls for is not an end in itself, but rather a means of helping us to express to one another and to Him the wonder of who He is and what He has done for us. Songs of the heart are an important means of helping us to realize that our God is always far better and far closer than we think He is. (Try it. Hum one of your favorite songs, in your heart, to the Lord right now.)

Let's not let our disagreements over music rob us of the music that God has given to lift our hearts to one another and to Him. If we must disagree, let's make sure that it is a gracious disagreement that doesn't stop the music.

Father in heaven, thank You for the gift of music. Please give us wisdom and love for one another as together with our parents, grandparents, children, and grandchildren, we cross the rough waters of changing culture.

Don't let us turn Your gift into an argument that will divide us. Give us a song in our own heart even when the music around us seems too fast or too slow, too new or too old.

September 2002

THE ATTITUDES OF CHRIST

WHAT IS THE GOAL OF spiritual maturity?

Jewish rabbis had their opinion. They did more than impart knowledge of the Torah and the Talmud. Their goal was to leave something of themselves in their students.

Ben Sirach, writing about 180 years before Christ, expresses the Jewish point of view when he says of a mature disciple: "When his father [teacher] dies, it is as though he is not dead. For he leaves behind him one like himself."

Christ had such a vision for His disciples (Luke 6:40). Even though He did not belong to a traditional school of thought, Jesus followed the rabbinic model by wanting His followers to share not only His knowledge but also His life and heart.

But what does it mean to be like Christ? What are the attitudes that mark us as His people? Let's test our understanding of what it means to be "conformed to the image" of Christ (Romans 8:29).

True or False?

Someone who is Christlike

1. Shows unlimited patience.
2. Doesn't get angry.
3. Refuses to be negative or critical.
4 Forgives everyone.
5. Tells all the truth, all the time.
6. Has a smile for every occasion.
7. Responds alike to all.
8. Avoids the company of unbelievers.
9. Condemns unprincipled people.
10. Speaks well of everyone.
11. Avoids conflict.
12. Is at peace with all.

In my view, these are all false impressions. Yet it's important for us to consider them. If we are not careful, we can make the mistake of thinking of our Lord as we might look at a statue of "the good shepherd" standing in the park.

The Many Attitudes of Christ

The Gospel accounts make it clear that our Lord was not unlimited in patience. On two occasions He turned over the tables of the money-changers in His Father's house (John 2:15; Matthew 21:12). He took issue with the self-centered attitudes of His friends (Matthew 20:20–28) and confronted religious leaders who were exploiting their followers (Matthew 23:1–39).

Although He never lied, He did not tell all of the truth to those who were not ready for it (John 2:24; Matthew 13:10–15). He wasn't always happy (Isaiah 53:1–4). Sometimes He cried (Luke 19:41; John 11:35; 12:27). He cared even for His enemies, but had a special affection for broken people who loved Him (Luke 6:27–36; John 14:21–23).

Even though no one could rightly accuse Him of wrong, He had a reputation for spending time with "public sinners" (Luke 7:34–39). He refused to condemn immoral people and reserved His harshest criticism for religious leaders who regularly condemned others (John 3:17; Matthew 15:7–14).

His followers considered Him a model of mental health, yet in His own day His enemies accused Him of being full of the devil, and His own friends and family thought He had gone mad (John 10:20; Mark 3:21).

One Phrase that Explains Many Attitudes

One of Jesus' disciples summarized the life of his Teacher with just a few words. According to John, the Rabbi who changed his life was "full of grace and truth" (John 1:14).

Every attitude our Lord expressed was rooted in a concern for others based on understanding. He healed, comforted, cried, taught, prayed, turned over the tables of the moneychangers, and confronted religious leaders because He understood the needs of others—and He cared. He spoke the truth with a heart of love.

The Process of Learning from Him

Those who sat around the table with Christ or who followed Him through the olive groves of Palestine got more than an education in Bible and doctrine. By spending time with Him they learned the spirit and heart of the law. They discovered that their Teacher's powerful miracles, short stories, and small acts of kindness were all designed to reshape not only their minds but also their hearts. With small, unsteady steps they gradually learned to love people more than money or power or reputation.

On the steps of the temple, on hot dusty roads, and in a storm-tossed boat, the men and women who spent time with Christ saw attitudes in Him that bridged the expanse between heaven and earth. In His eyes they saw not only reflections of His Father but of the people He loved.

Today we still learn His attitudes as His disciples did—in His presence. Through the windows of the Gospels we watch the Teacher of teachers gather His students around and say to them: Blessed are those who see their spiritual need, who mourn their self-centeredness, and who surrender their hearts to God so as to be useful and helpful to others (Matthew 5:1–10).

The apostle Paul expressed the same attitudes in different words when he wrote: "Let nothing be done through selfish ambition or conceit, but in lowliness of mind let each esteem others better than himself. Let each of you look out not only for his own interests, but also for the interests of others. Let this mind be in you which was also in Christ Jesus" (Philippians 2:3–5).

Spiritual maturity is more than learning to do the right thing. It's more than asking, "What would Jesus do?" Christlike attitudes require us to ask, "Who and what would Jesus care about?"

There is a well-worn saying that deserves to be heard again: "Others won't care how much we know until we show them how much we care."

Father in heaven, all too often we've been people with an attitude that doesn't reflect the likeness of Your Son. Please do through us what we haven't been able to do for ourselves. Let us reflect the mind and attitudes of Your Son—for Your honor, for His sake, for our need, and for the good of all who know us.

December 2003

WISDOM

ACCORDING TO BUDDHIST FOLKLORE, two traveling monks reached a river where they met a young woman. Wary of the current, she asked if they could carry her across. One of the monks hesitated, but the other quickly picked her up onto his shoulders, transported her across the water, and put her down on the other bank. She thanked him and departed.

As the monks continued on their way, the one was brooding and preoccupied. Finally, unable to hold his silence, he said, "Brother, our spiritual training teaches us to avoid any contact with women, but you picked that one up on your shoulders and carried her!"

"Brother," the second monk replied, "I set her down on the other side, while you are still carrying her."

A Question of Wisdom

The insight of the second monk raises an interesting question for followers of Christ. If we acknowledge examples of moral and spiritual insight in another religion, do we weaken our case for the distinctiveness of our own faith?

I ask the question because I believe we actually strengthen our case by seeing that one of the things the Bible does is help us see wisdom outside of its own pages. By being our inspired standard for wisdom, the Bible shows how to recognize (1) natural, (2) religious, and (3) moral insights in the world around us. Most important, the Scriptures show us how these first three kinds of wisdom can help us see our need for (4) the redemptive wisdom of the cross.

Let's take a closer look at how the first three kinds of wisdom can help us build bridges to those outside of our faith, without compromising the distinctiveness of Christ in the process.

Natural Wisdom

The Old Testament book of Proverbs gives us examples of practical insights that abound in the cultures and religions of the world. Solomon's wisdom shows us how to learn from the animals, from agriculture, and from personal reflection on how life works. Many of his wise sayings illustrate the value of a natural wisdom that can also be found in other religions.

> Wise is the one who is not too big to learn from the ant (Proverbs 6:6–8).

> The most important battles are fought in the mind (Proverbs 16:32; 25:28).

A benefit of such natural wisdom is that it can help anyone live a more thoughtful life. A downside is that natural wisdom does not by itself give us hope in a world where all of our accomplishments are subject to change and loss (Ecclesiastes 1:1–11).

Religious Wisdom

People of many cultures have found it difficult to think that the wonders of the natural world have no counterpart on the other side of death. As a result, many religions have tried to give their followers hope beyond the grave. While the following quotes are from the Bible, they have parallels in other religious systems.

> Those who hope only in this life are destined for despair (Ecclesiastes 2:15–20).

> Nothing is more relevant than the eternal (Ecclesiastes 12:13–14).

By believing in life after death, people of many religions have found courage to make sacrifices for a better world beyond. But eternal perspectives have also been a problem. By minimizing the importance of this life, many have wasted the earth's resources, waged unnecessary wars, and sacrificed their lives at the expense of others. Religious wisdom does not make people good merely by offering the hope of immortality.

Moral Wisdom

From Moses to Jesus, the Scriptures show that spirituality without morality can result in everything from false gods to religious exploitation of the poor. According to the Bible, moral wisdom is so important that our Creator wrote His laws not only in stone, but also in our hearts (Romans 2:14–15). The result is that the Bible resonates with a universal human conscience when it says things like,

Do to others as you would have them do to you (Matthew 7:12).

Don't return evil for evil but overcome evil with good (Romans 12:21).

Once again, however, we are faced with an insight that is incomplete. When we think about the moral wisdom of love, our problem is not so much in knowing but in doing. No matter how much we want to love, we easily slide into self-centered thinking that causes us to hurt and be hurt. None of us gives or receives as much love as our hearts long for.

Redemptive Wisdom

Because we are all wounded people, we need more than natural, religious, and moral wisdom to do the right thing. We need a redemptive insight to help us deal with the wrongs we have done to others and that others have done to us.

This was the kind of wisdom Jesus offered when He stepped into our broken world and said, "Come to Me, all you who labor and are heavy laden, and I will give you rest" (Matthew 11:28).

Those who are well don't need a doctor, but those who are sick. I have not come to call good people, but sinners to repentance (Mark 2:17).

Christ's invitation to hurting, helpless people was not new. For centuries, Jewish prophets had been declaring that the Most High God lives not only in the heavens but also in the dark valleys of crushed and shattered people who recognize their desperate need of Him (Psalm 34:18; Isaiah 57:15).

What was new with Christ was that at the crossroads of the world, and on the center page of human history, God unveiled the secret of His redemptive wisdom. By an act of immeasurable love, our Creator became our substitute, dying in our place for our sin (1 Corinthians 1:17–31).

Wisdom doesn't get more profound than this. The darkest, most tragic moment of human history became the means by which our Creator could offer us the light of His Spirit, His forgiveness, and His everlasting life.

By the redemptive wisdom of Christ, wasted, ruined, and hopeless people learn to love as they have been loved, to forgive as they have been forgiven, and to salvage as they have been salvaged.

Father in heaven, Your Son is known for rescuing the kind of people we are inclined to condemn. Something has gone terribly wrong. Please don't let us rest until we too are showing every day, and in every way, the redemptive wisdom of the cross.

September 2004

THE PATH TO PEACE

THE SCREENSAVER ON MY computer is a daily reminder of one of the most important thoughts I've ever had. When my laptop has been inactive for a few minutes, the screen goes black. Then large red words begin scrolling across the display saying, "The only way to peace of mind is to see each day as an opportunity to trust God and love people."

More than a few times, this reminder to see every circumstance as an opportunity for what matters has softened my anxiety and cooled my anger. I'm also convinced that even though my screensaver is not a direct quote of Scripture, it reflects the heart of Paul's jailhouse letter to the Philippians. Penned in the discomfort of a lock-up, while former friends accused him of being a threat to society, Paul laid the foundation for the thought that keeps changing my mind and my life. He called it "the peace of God, which surpasses all understanding" (Philippians 4:7).

Where can we find this peace?

What we know about this peace is that it does not insulate us from concern or loss. Neither will it spare us the internal struggle of emotions rooted in the fragile chemistry of our own bodies.

The peace Paul described is a deep, stabilizing peace of faith that comes as a gift from the Spirit of God. It is calmness of soul that enables us to be sure of the goodness and presence of God even when emotions are whispering and screaming like demons. As an assurance of priceless value, this peace is more of a "knowing" than a "feeling."

It is at this point that we need to be careful. Although the peace of God is a gift of His Spirit, there are some choices we need to make at three levels of our life.

First Level. On the surface, real issues threaten our peace of mind. Because our natural inclination is to let these surface issues rob us of our peace of mind, Paul gave us two lines of defense. First, he encouraged us to bring all of our concerns and requests to God in order to experience a peace that goes beyond our ability to understand (Philippians 4:6–7).

Second, he urged us to refocus our thoughts by thinking about what is true, and good, and honorable. He immediately went on to say that if we follow his example, the God of peace will be with us (Philippians 4:8–9).

Until recently I misunderstood the second of these two strategies. I assumed that when he urged us to think about what is true and honest and good Paul was saying, in effect: If you want peace of mind, think good thoughts. Be positive. Be optimistic. Don't think the worst. Think the best about people and life.

Looking back, I should have known better. Avoidance was not Paul's style. When he focused his own mind on what is true, and pure, and praiseworthy, he faced his own failures. He went to the rescue of others. He cared to the point of tears. He was realistic about human evil. He understood the strategies of demons.

Even in his letter to the Philippians, Paul openly faced disappointments, conflicts, and facts that made him cry (Philippians 3:18). Understanding what Paul meant by "honorable thinking" helps us to see that he was advocating a peace that can be experienced with God in the middle of our problems rather than apart from them.

Second Level. Below the surface, unseen motives shape our responses. All of us live with subsurface obstacles to peace. Everything we do is with an unseen motive that, in many cases, we'd rather not think about. In everything we get involved with, we have a self-centered personal interest that can rob us of our peace of mind and make us seem dangerous to those around us.

It is because of these natural inclinations that Paul urged us to let God override our natural inclinations with the spirit of His love. Paul knew that without heartfelt concern for others there can be no lasting peace.

What I failed to see for a long time, however, is that it doesn't do any good to say something like, "For your own peace of mind, and for goodness' sake, start loving and caring for one another." Moral emphasis is not the solution. God doesn't ask us to have right motives because it is the right thing to do. He asks us to love one another on the basis of "underlying foundational issues."

Third Level. At a still deeper level, foundational beliefs shape our motives. Just as there is at least one unseen motive behind every action, so every motive rests on an underlying foundation of belief or misbelief.

Our natural tendency is to believe our eyes or our desires. We are most inclined to assess our well-being by counting our natural resources. We are quick to count our money and our friends, or to check our blood pressure and cholesterol to form a belief about how we are doing.

From his prison cell, however, Paul gave us a different example. He urged us to believe that the Lord is present (Philippians 4:5), that God Himself can give us a peace we can't understand (Philippians 4:7), and that our Provider God can be our source of well-being in all the circumstances of life (Philippians 4:13, 19). Even in his repeated appeals for good and honorable motives (Philippians 2:3–4), Paul made it clear that an honest concern for others must emerge from our own belief that our God is attentively looking after our every need.

This confidence in God was the secret of Paul's peace of mind (Philippians 4:11–13). This foundational reliance upon his Provider is what allowed him to say to others of like faith, "I can do all things through Christ who strengthens me. And my God shall supply all your need according to His riches in glory by Christ Jesus" (Philippians 4:13, 19).

Father in heaven, in so many ways we have looked for contentment in all of the wrong places. We have counted our well-being in terms of our strengths rather than in the weaknesses that have brought us back to You. Help us to rely on You, Lord. Please give us a peace that we can know even when we don't feel it.

August 2001

RANDOM ACTS

To AN ANGRY WORLD marked increasingly by random acts of violence, the bumper sticker on the car in front of me said, "Do random acts of kindness."

Thinking this is the kind of attitude that could make the world a better place, I recall wondering about the spiritual orientation of the driver. It occurred to me that the car could have been driven by an atheist, a New Ager, or a follower of Christ.

What eventually got under my skin, however, was the realization that by acting on such thoughts, many non-Christians live better lives than I do.

Many without a personal relationship with Christ are better for the neighborhood and better for the community. Many who are not yet on their way to heaven are better for the environment our Savior created, and better for the troubled and helpless members of society our Father cares about.

What hurts the most is that those of us who have raised our hand for heaven are sometimes identified with the hate-groups of society.

Sometimes, of course, the accusation that Christians are angry, intolerant, and even violent is the result of misunderstanding. Church history reminds us that some of the first Christians were also mistakenly accused of being idolaters, cannibals, homosexuals, and adulterers. Some outsiders misunderstood the church's practice of symbolically "eating and drinking" the body and blood of Christ. Others misunderstood the practice of brotherly love. Still others mistakenly thought it was impossible to worship Jesus as God without doing damage to historic Jewish monotheism.

In some cases today, though, we may need to take responsibility for misleading those who misunderstand us. Sometimes some of us do fit the profile of a counterculture group that is angry with a government or media we think is undermining our values.

There is a time for anger. There is a time to act against the sewer rats that are spreading disease among our children. But even then we can't afford to let our anger become so frequent as to override our love.

I'm convinced that some of us don't even realize the place we have given to anger. Are we impatient with a young generation that has no respect for authority? Are we disgusted with neighbors who are living together without being married? Are we fed up with educators who teach godless evolution as if it were a proven fact? Are we impatient with religious people who don't believe as we do? Are we critical of unchurched people who treat Sunday like every other day of the week?

And who appears to be more Christlike? Who appears to be the more noble example? Is it the Bible-believer fed up with society's evils? Or is it the agnostic committed to being surprisingly good to unsuspecting people.

I write this after being personally convicted by the New Testament letter to Titus. More than once, the apostle Paul encouraged Titus to teach others to show by their actions that they were authentic followers of Christ. Over and over, Paul makes it clear that our Lord is not asking us merely to be good, but to be good for something.

Paul wrote, "This is a faithful saying, and these things I want you to affirm constantly, that those who have believed in God should be careful to maintain good works. These things are good and profitable to men" (Titus 3:8; see also Titus 2:7, 10, 14; 3:1–2, 14).

But, the cornered little man in me argues, what if I don't have the means to do random acts of kindness? What if I don't have the money to be the kind of gift-giver I'd like to be? What if I can't afford to become the community benefactor?

To that my conscience responds. Yes, sure would be nice to have millions to share. But some of the most needed acts of kindness can be done with small amounts of time, and with the kind of pocket money that can either be wasted or put to good use.

With embarrassment I admit to myself that a short note expressing interest and encouragement can often do far more than a material offer of help. I can't deny that sometimes it is simply the unexpected smile, the thoughtful courtesy, the eye contact, the remembered name, the most basic thoughtfulness that helps others to feel cared for and honored.

How we "bankroll" this needed Christlikeness isn't the issue. God, the Giver of everything that comes into our lives, is able to orchestrate and support the random and planned acts of kindness that help us to live like His Son in this world.

Father, I know words are cheap. But I want to be different. I'm willing to change. I need You to give me the presence of mind and freedom of Spirit to reflect Your giving heart.

Please direct another clean-up of my life. Show me today how to let Your Son live His life through me to those who desperately need a touch from You. I want others to find Your love in the place of my anger.

December 1998

COMPETITION

IS IT CHRISTIAN TO BE competitive? Can a player, coach, or fan go for a league championship and still be counted among those who "look out not only for [their] own interests, but also for the interests of others" (Philippians 2:4)?

The issue is bigger than team sports. It is difficult to live in this world without "doing battle" for something, with someone, at least some of the time. In free-market economies, democratic elections, and educational grading systems, competition is everywhere. From Super Bowls to Sunday school "sword drills," rivalry makes life interesting.

Too often, though, the playing fields become killing fields. Bitter rivalries in sports, business, and government can degenerate into blood-sport, dominance, and cutthroat pursuit of money and influence.

Advocates of free markets reason that the struggle for limited resources is simply the result of being the kind of people we are in the kind of world in which we find ourselves. They reason that while competition can bring out the worst in us, it can also bring out the best.

To its backers, healthy competition is rooted in cooperation. Friendly rivalry not only improves quality of goods and services, it also provides recreation, entertainment, jobs, and family incomes. In business as in sports, opponents can agree to play by the book for common interests. Competitive sports can be used to teach cooperation, hard work, concentration, creativity, integrity, self-discipline, endurance, grace in defeat, and goodwill in victory.

But is the competitive spirit good from a Christian point of view? Could Jesus have enjoyed a hard-fought game on the playing fields of Nazareth? I think so.

What we know for sure is that Jesus taught us to love one another, and the apostle James wrote that selfish ambition and bitter rivalry are sources of all kinds of evil (James 3:14–16), yet the apostle Paul also used athletic competition to illustrate Christian living (1 Corinthians 9:24–27). He likened a follower of Christ to an athlete who strives to win while playing by the rules.

The Scriptures seem to indicate that whether competition is healthy or dangerous depends not only on how we play the game but also on why we are competing. The Bible shows us that below the surface of all rivalries are unseen motives and underlying beliefs. If those motives and beliefs are rooted only in our own interests, we cannot rightly claim to be competing in the spirit of Christ. If, on the other hand, our motives are to test one another for mutual interests and enjoyment, we may be able to give 100 percent to the battle while showing Christlike goodwill in victory and grace in defeat.

Even more helpful to me has been the discovery that real security is not found in winning but in learning to trust our Provider God.

Such provision and competition were at the heart of the temptation of Christ (Matthew 4:1–11). On a battlefield in the Judean wilderness, two opponents stood face to face. Their rivalry was strong. The fallen angel of darkness tried to match wits with a physically weakened Son of Man (Matthew 4:2). Person to person, will to will they faced off—with our futures going to the winner.

Three times the devil tried to get Jesus' eyes off the prize. Three times the adversary tried to get the Son of God to trade our lives for a short-lived taste of power or glory. Each time, Jesus saw the challenge as a test of His dependence on His Father. When tempted to use undue force, break the rules, or cut corners to satisfy shortsighted goals, Jesus remained faithful. He refused to take matters into His own hands (Matthew 4:4), didn't try to force the hand of the Father (Matthew 4:5–7), and didn't bow His knee to a rival sovereign (Matthew 4:8–11).

With mental toughness, physical endurance, and grace, Jesus showed that maintaining dependence on God is more important than a short-lived show of dominance.

Father in heaven, we have not been as wise as Your Son. Forgive us for using the pressures of competition as an excuse to break the rules of dependence on You. Please show us how to give as much strength to the struggle as Your Son did, and to do it with His ability to trust You for the outcome.

Teach us to keep our eyes on the prize of Your approval, and on the trophy of real people loved into Your presence.

May 1997

COURTESIES

COURTESIES. I EXTEND courtesies to God. I politely thank Him for a good meal and a good day. I thank Him as I thank a waiter for filling up my cup with coffee. I thank Him as I tip for service well done.

Yet sometimes I don't feel like leaving a tip or giving thanks. I don't always feel thankful because I don't always feel well served. All too often I don't wake up in the morning overwhelmed by God's goodness and overflowing with a heart that knows life is good and that heaven is far better.

What's wrong? Don't I know the halls of heaven throb with the music and praise of adoring creatures? Yes. But this isn't heaven. I agree with those who have noted that it's hard to think about heaven when your stomach's empty. I'm not starving. But sometimes it feels like there's a hole in my heart.

Some of my most deeply felt prayers for others are not answered. Deep problems linger. Uncertainty about the future robs me of gratefulness. When I thank God for the good He does, I cannot forget what He has withheld.

What's wrong with me? Why don't I feel that with every waking breath and thought I owe God unending, heartfelt praise? Gradually I begin to realize that I have slipped into the presumption that God owes me something. I act as if I deserve what I get, and more. I didn't ask to be born. Don't I deserve a good meal, a car that runs well, meaningful work, and friends to count on? Don't I deserve health and happiness, and all of the good things God gives me? That's why sometimes I say "thanks." I don't want to seem ungrateful.

Once in a while the fog lifts long enough for me to see a different picture. In those moments I am amazed to see the truth about what God owes me. Nothing. He doesn't owe me anything. Not health, or life, or peace of mind. He doesn't owe me friendships, or meaningful work, or money for extras. Whether I like it or not, God doesn't owe me answers to my prayers, or the conviction that all will be well with the souls that are breaking my heart. God owes me nothing.

More accurately, I don't even deserve what I have been given, let alone what God has withheld. I don't deserve another day, another meal, another laugh. God is not indebted to me. He has no obligation to make me happy by giving me what my heart demands. He is not beholden to me just because He made me.

Thinking I deserve anything is my unholy presumption. I often forget the most basic and foundational doctrines of Christian faith. I forget that "grace" means "undeserved help." "Mercy" means "undeserved relief." What do we have that has not first been received as "grace" or "mercy"? Together they encompass everything. I deserve nothing. Any good is an act of God's sheer, undeserved kindness.

In my presumption I have it all wrong. God owes me nothing. But I owe Him everything.

Thank You, Lord, for shoes to put on my feet, for feet to move, and for a blood-spattered cross at which to stand. Thank You for graciously and lovingly leading us to the ground at the foot of the cross where Your Son died. We don't deserve to stand on such holy ground. I don't deserve such love. I don't deserve His suffering, or His offer of forgiveness and eternal life. But You, Father, You deserve praise. Together with Your Son and Spirit, You deserve our unending thanks, and honor, and worship. Thank You for all You have done.

February 1996

GOING TO CHURCH

I WISH I COULD SAY THAT going to church is always a good experience for me. It isn't. Even though I'm a member of a warm and accepting church family, time in church often leaves me cold. Sometimes I don't feel good about those around me. My emotions feel distant during the pastoral prayer. My voice is flat and lifeless during congregational singing.

Sometimes I feel alone even among so many. In those moments the public reading of the Word of God echoes around me but not in me. Even a strong pastoral message seems weak and distant. After the final prayer, I'm relieved to get out as quickly as possible.

On other occasions, my experience is just the opposite. Going to church can be like going home. In the quietness of the sanctuary and in the purpose of the hour, I have profound and clear thoughts. I feel far more alive and focused than during the rest of the week. The Lord seems near. Sometimes I breathe in church a kind of grace that seems to be reserved for family gatherings.

What is the difference? How can times of worship provide such extremes of experience? I'm not sure. It doesn't seem as simple as whether or not I have gone to church with the right attitude. Sometimes I come warm and leave cold. At other times I come cold and leave warm.

Those are the unpredictable feelings that play like unruly children in the presence of another more difficult issue. More troubling yet is our changing habit of church attendance. Why are more and more of us going to church less and less? It's not as though we could plead ignorance. Who in the family doesn't know that our Father has told us to meet together to encourage one another to love and good works—and to do so more and more as we see the day of His coming approaching? (Hebrews 10:25).

How can we do less and less of the very thing our Lord has told us to do more and more?

Don't get me wrong. I can't find any place in Scripture that says a godly person will always enjoy being with the Lord's people. Neither can I find any statement that says a child of God should be in church every time the doors are open. What I do find, and cannot explain away, is a statement that clearly says we have reason "to not forsake the assembling of ourselves together," but to meet together to encourage acts of faith and love, and to do so more and more as we see the Day approaching.

Lord, forgive us for doing less of what You have told us to do more. Please give us, in the time that remains, a heart for the people of Your body . . . and ears for the thoughts of Your heart.

August 1995

STREET TALK

SOME OF THE MOST IMPORTANT thoughts we have ever had are routinely profaned in common language.

The language of profanity is an eye-opener. "Oh, my God!" "Hell." "Damn!" "For God's sake!" "Jesus Christ!" "Oh, my Lord!"

As I've taken a closer look at my own heart, I've realized that my inner inclination for unspoken profanity isn't merely an unfortunate reflection of the culture. Neither are my own thoughts merely silent echoes of someone else's verbal indiscretions.

Neither can I claim that the use of inappropriate language is someone else's problem just because I'm careful not to let such thoughts out in public. The profane expressions others shamelessly use find unexpressed resonance in my own feelings of anger, anxiety, or arrogance.

I have come to realize that even the unspoken language of profanity gives me red flags of the soul. These words never signal a submissive relationship with the Father. They never show grace. And in my experience, the near-miss substitutes of "heck," "darn," or "gosh" are also indicators of concern. Flirting with "holy cow" or "holy Moses" might seem cute. But I've also had to ask myself, "Where is this coming from?" Why not use the names of politicians, entertainers, or athletes? What is the emotional draw that has inspired a whole series of sound-alike "gol darn," "gees," and "gee whiz"?

Why do those of us who know enough not to say the real thing still feel a need to exclaim "for cripes sake," "oh, my gosh," or "what the heck"? A dictionary of slang shows that to use such phrases, whether knowingly or not, is flirting with profanity.

Why pursue such a moralistic subject? Not to try to fix myself with the law of forbidden language. Knowing that such common language is inappropriate is actually what helps to make it such a "perfect way" to express emotions that are already disconnected from grace.

No. Let's not use our embarrassing inner inclinations to beat ourselves up. Let's use these profane impulses as an occasion to think about what's happening inside us and to awaken us to our need of the grace of submission. Let's use our unspoken inclinations as an occasion to think about our need for the One whose Spirit we are inclined to insult.

Honesty about our inner impulses is a good occasion to think about the ever-present One whose nearness captures even the most irreligious among us with "Oh, my God!"

Think about the expressions "for Christ's sake," and "for God's sake." What thoughts are more profound or needed? There is no more lofty motive than to lovingly act for the honor and sake of God Himself. Think how many workdays would be changed if employees were convinced that for God's sake they would do their work for His honor. Imagine how many marriages could be saved and children loved if parents would act not merely out of their own interest, but more so for the interests and reputation and name of God. For God's sake.

So how should we react when we hear someone else use profanity? Should we agree to a crusade to make those who use the name of God irreverently pay for their insult? I doubt that it would be wise or Christlike. Profanity is merely a symptom of deeper issues.

If we do speak up, let's do so with gentleness and humility. Our response to profanity is no occasion for self-righteousness. I can't tell how many times I've found the same language rising from within me. Unspoken. But thought. And felt. Within me. A mark of my own flesh. A reason for me to ask, "What's happening here? Why am I using language that is typical of those who don't know Jesus as the Son of God?"

The answer, in principle, may be the same for us as for non-Christian users. It is when we are not living in the awareness of the presence of God, when we are living without gratitude, and when we instead are filled with our own nervous anxiety that we are apt to use profane language.

Father, forgive me for taking Your Name in vain, even if only within the silence of my own heart. Help all of us to recognize the nervous self-reliance that causes us to use such high thoughts in such a low and vulgar way. Help us to learn from our own profanity to see our need of a filling of Your Spirit so that we instead will say, "Oh, my God, let everything that I do be not for my own satisfaction and self-serving motives but rather for Christ's sake."

September 1998

THE IMMUNE SYSTEM

AFTER READING AN ADVISORY about disease risks for travelers, I visited our Community Health Service to get updated on immunizations. Actually, my wife told me to go down and get my shots (smile).

During the visit, the clinic nurse asked me how long I was going to be out of the country. She said anyone who travels internationally repeatedly, or for any length of time, is at special risk of disease. "Seasoned" travelers, she went on to say, are apt to become careless about their food and water.

Before leaving the clinic, I rolled up my sleeves and took two shots in each arm. Four doses of "inactivated cells" were injected into my veins. The principle of immunization, as I understand it, is that the body doesn't see the difference between dead and living cells. When the serum is injected, our body begins to build up a defense system against the real thing.

Another Side of Inoculation

As with almost everything else in life, immunizations can have side effects. After getting my shots, I talked to a friend who said he didn't like the idea of having "swamp water" put in his veins. Even though serum is not "swamp water," I knew what he was talking about. In a small percentage of cases, inoculations are followed by complications. Because of such remote but real risks, I had to read and sign a paper at the Health Department indicating that I understood the potential dangers.

There is, however, another danger of "inoculation" the Health Department didn't warn me about. I wouldn't expect them to. The danger is spiritual and is related only in principle to "shots of dead cells" that make us resistant to the real thing. It is the kind of subtle inoculation that causes us to say, "familiarity breeds contempt."

This natural resistance that develops with time shows up in the last book of the Bible. The book of Revelation is addressed to seven churches at the end of the first century. These congregations probably included second and third generation believers who had been on the road for a while. A few decades of church history were in the books. The members of these churches would have had a fair amount of history on one another, and on their Lord as well.

The "spiritual honeymoon" was over. Familiarity was at work. Five out of seven congregations had carelessly become infected with life-threatening diseases of the spirit. From "a loss of first love" to "the cooling effects of material success," these veteran churches were becoming resistant to one another, to their Lord, and to the needs around them.

The pattern of five out of seven life-threatening conditions puts me off balance. The percentage runs against what I'd like to believe. I'd rather believe that time, knowledge, and experience are all working for us. I'd rather believe that our familiarity with the issues of faith is making us resistant to diseases of the soul.

Inoculation in Reverse

What I see in these churches, in history, and in myself is a kind of immunity that works against health rather than for it. What child, neighbor, or acquaintance of religion doesn't run the risk of getting injected with the "dead cells" of familiarity?

Given enough disappointment with people of faith, who among us isn't inclined to build up immunities to the real thing? Given enough knowledge of the failures of others, who among us isn't inclined to focus more on the failures of believers than on the Lord of the church Himself?

Inoculation in Surprising Places

But before assuming that spiritual immunity is only about the failures of people like us, let's remember that the family and neighbors of Jesus also used "time and familiarity" to take Him for granted. Even those who lived in the same neighborhood as the Son of God were inclined to dismiss Him with the excuse, "Oh, Him! I know Him. I know His father, His mother, His brothers and sisters" (John 6:42).

Seeing that familiarity could breed contempt even for the Son of God helps us keep matters in perspective. We can be inoculated not only by the real failures of people of faith, but also by what we take for granted. We can wrongly assume that we are seeing the whole picture. We can blame God for the wrongs of others. We can even suppose that because heaven doesn't strike us dead for our self-centered choices our Lord isn't watching, or concerned, or grieving, or angry.

Inoculation Has an Antidote

Thankfully, there is an antidote to reverse our human tendency. Christ offers this remedy to the aging churches of the Revelation when He asks them to take another look at Him.

Each personal message begins with a carefully selected word picture of Himself. Part of the implication is, "Stop looking at everyone else! Look at Me!"

Then, while reminding them that He Himself is the beginning and end of their journey (Revelation 1:8), He reminds them of the wonder of His power, the power of His presence, and the renewing presence of His Spirit.

Father, please forgive me for taking You, Your Son, and Your renewing Spirit for granted. Even though I know better, I've acted as if You were predictable, and as if my ways were Your ways.

Wake me up, Lord! Again and again, please wake us up! Let us see Your goodness in every new sunrise, in the cry of the hurting people around us, and in the timeless words of Your Book. Let us walk with You today as if being shown a world we have never seen before, by an Owner, Father, and King we have just begun to know.

July 2001

PEOPLE-WATCHING

A PEOPLE WATCHER DEFINES his sport like this: "The art of people-watching involves studying the subjects, guessing who they are, where they are coming from, and where they are going. Sometimes it even includes trying to imagine what they are thinking."

What rings true about this description is that it describes people-watching as a series of guesses rather than a science. This is especially true when it comes to issues of spiritual identity. Jesus Himself taught that it may be impossible to distinguish those who know Him from those who don't (Matthew 13:24–30).

Why is spiritual identification so difficult? Let's take a closer look at some of the factors that sometimes make children of God as hard to identify as just-hatched baby birds.

Disappointment with God

After the God of the Bible rescued His chosen people from the slave yards of Egypt, the Jewish nation danced to the music of celebration. But when the same children of Israel found themselves in a barren wilderness marked by too little water and too many scorpions, their songs turned into growls of complaint and unrest.

Some of us have found ourselves in similar circumstances. When our disillusionment cools into bitterness and hopelessness, any family resemblance to Jesus is difficult to see (Hebrews 12:15).

Distraction

When the chosen people finally made it to the Promised Land, they encountered another problem. Before long, they found that distraction in good times is as dangerous as disillusionment in times of pain. In a land flowing with milk and honey, the children of Israel did not have to decide consciously to turn away from their God. All they needed to do was to be absorbed and preoccupied with all they had been given. Before long, they were like wandering sheep who didn't know how dependent they were on their shepherd (Isaiah 53:6).

Dangerous Relationships

Herd instinct can be dangerous, especially when the lead animal is lost. Sheep have been known to follow one another off a cliff. So have people. Many years after Israel's wilderness wanderings, the apostle Paul would write, "Do not be misled: 'Bad company corrupts good character.' Come back to your senses as you ought, and stop sinning" (1 Corinthians 15:33–34 NIV).

Unchanged Tendencies

If the Bible urges us to do something, it is because we are inclined to do just the opposite. Our capacity to be self-centered remains unchanged (Romans 7:14–25). The downward pull of desire remains as predictable as the law of gravity. Whenever we stop living under the influence of the Spirit and the Word of God (Galatians 5:16–26), it becomes as natural for us to revert to self-interest as for a kite to drift slowly to earth when the wind stops blowing.

Self-Reliance

On the night of Jesus' arrest, one of His closest followers, a tough-minded fisherman named Peter, announced that he was ready to follow his teacher to prison or to death (Luke 22:33). Within a few hours, Peter denied repeatedly that he even knew the man from Galilee. His failure reminds us that even the original disciples of Christ learned about the danger of self-reliance the hard way.

Prayerlessness

One reason Peter was blindsided by self-reliance was that, at a critical moment, he did not enter into a prayerful dependence on God. Neither Peter nor his friends responded when Jesus urged, "Watch and pray, lest you enter into temptation. The spirit indeed is willing, but the flesh is weak" (Matthew 26:41). Instead, the disciples slept. Years later, a New Testament writer penned a letter that linked prayerlessness to some of the most destructive kinds of spiritual failure (James 4:1–6).

Carelessness

King David was a man after God's own heart (Acts 13:22). His record of spiritual accomplishments, however, did not keep him from becoming an adulterer and murderer. One night, as others fought his battles, and as he stood in apparent security on his own palace rooftop, David used the power of his office to pursue another man's wife. In an unguarded moment, David discovered the meaning of the statement, "Let him who thinks he stands take heed lest he fall" (1 Corinthians 10:12).

An Unexamined Heart

In the moment of temptation, the human heart can be a master of excuses. In the rush of desire, our minds are adept at coming up with ways of making wrong look right. That's probably why the prophet Jeremiah wrote, "The heart is deceitful above all things, and desperately wicked; who can know it?" (Jeremiah 17:9).

Unseen Enemies

If we belong to Christ, we have a spiritual enemy who knows how to stir up and exploit our desires. Over the centuries, he has claimed many victims. While he can't make us sin, Satan and his demons are constantly looking for weaknesses that give them an inroad into our lives (Ephesians 4:27; 6:10–20). Like predatory animals, they look for vulnerable prey (1 Peter 5:8). They would like us to forget that we are at war and that we have every reason to be watching for their next attempt to neutralize us.

A Lack of Interdependence

The apostle Paul likened followers of Christ to a human body where all members are dependent on one another (1 Corinthians 12). While we may have reasons for not wanting to be dependent on others, such an attitude does not reflect the spirit of Christ. He made it clear that He calls us not only to Himself, but also to one another (Hebrews 10:24–25). On our own, we lack the variety of strengths and abilities that are necessary to keep us from being reabsorbed into a materialistic, self-centered existence.

These ten factors give us some reasons why people-watching is not an exact science. They may also help us understand why the apostle Paul wrote, " 'The Lord knows those who are His,' and, 'Let everyone who names the name of Christ depart from [unrighteousness]' " (2 Timothy 2:19).

Father in heaven, You know our hearts so much better than we do. Forgive us for judging others while taking our own relationship with You for granted. Please help us to rise above the factors that keep us from distinguishing ourselves as Your children.

February 2006

CONTENTMENT

WHAT IS THE SECRET OF contentment? Thoughtful people have offered many suggestions. What follows are pieces of advice I've picked up along the way. When considered alone, each perspective is only a part of the picture. When considered together with the Word of God, they combine to show that while contentment is not always a virtue, it is always an option.

Accept What You Cannot Change

The prayer is well-known: "God, grant me the serenity to accept the things I cannot change, the courage to change the things I can, and the wisdom to know the difference." With this goal as a guiding star, many have found peace in the middle of chaotic and stormy circumstances. It is advice that parallels the teaching of Jesus, who asked His disciples, "Who of you by worrying can add a single hour to his life?" (Luke 12:25 NIV).

Put a Price on What You Already Have

Someone has said, "There are two ways to be rich. One is to have all you want. The other is to be satisfied with what you have." While some would consider such a comment bad for the economy, I remember the words of a friend who observed, "I have found that the desire to have is soon replaced by the fear of losing." He echoed the words of Solomon, who said, "When goods increase, they increase who eat them" (Ecclesiastes 5:11), and "Better a handful with quietness than both hands full, together with toil and grasping for the wind" (Ecclesiastes 4:6).

Be Realistic about Expectations

Some have linked dissatisfaction to frustrated expectation. According to them, "Unhappiness is not found in what we experience, but in what we expect." Pushed to an extreme, "Nothing is more discouraging than to expect 'heaven' now." With this truth in mind, someone has wisely observed, "The only way to find satisfaction is to have this expectation: Each day is an opportunity to delight in the Lord."

Put Trouble to Work for You

Consider these sayings: "The happy person is the one who can enjoy the scenery when taking a detour," and, "The pessimist sees the difficulty in every opportunity. The optimist sees opportunity in every difficulty."

Paul gave us his own example of someone who in terrible circumstances found that what is good about weakness is that it gives an occasion to depend on the strength of God. "Therefore I take pleasure in infirmities, in reproaches, in needs, in persecutions, in distresses, for Christ's sake. For when I am weak, then I am strong" (2 Corinthians 12:10).

Have Confidence in a Wise Provider

Through the ages many have found contentment in a simple belief: "When God is all you have, you will find that He is all you need." For that reason the New Testament says, "Let your conduct be without covetousness; be content with such things as you have. For He Himself has said, 'I will never leave you, nor forsake you'" (Hebrews 13:5).

Know What to Be Content About

Contentment is not always desirable. According to the Bible, there's no virtue in being satisfied with this world, with our own accomplishments, or even with the approval of others. Neither is there honor in contentment that is not combined with due diligence and wise counsel. The Scripture urges us to improve our circumstances by good planning and hard work. It calls us to doggedly pursue knowledge and understanding.

The contentment the Bible calls for is more specific than general. The Spirit of Christ urges us to be satisfied with circumstances we cannot change without violating principles of love, faith, and an appropriate hope in heaven. To this end the apostle Paul wrote, "I have learned in whatever state I am, to be content" (Philippians 4:11).

Know What Wise Contentment Looks Like

As we have already seen, the acceptance Paul found did not come without pain or distress. When he said he had learned to be content, he also admitted to pain and bother: "I know how to be abased, and I know how to abound. Everywhere and in all things I have learned both to be full and to be hungry, both to abound and to suffer need. I can do all things through Christ who strengthens me. Nevertheless you have done well that you shared in my distress" (Philippians 4:12–14).

While godly contentment is comforting, it is not the same thing as comfort. It does not assure a general peace of mind. What it does do is express a conviction that God has a right to test our hearts with much or little. As painful and overwhelming as physical needs can be, Paul discovered that he would rather suffer hardship while going to the rescue of others than to be concerned only about himself.

So what is the contentment we should long for? Not comfort. Not wealth. Not satisfaction with our own accomplishments. Not contentment with the world around us. But a learned conviction about the goodness, faithfulness, and sufficiency of our Provider.

August 1997

AESOP

UNTIL RECENTLY, I THOUGHT of Aesop as an ancient Dr. Seuss. Then I started reading his fables. What surprised me is that his stories about talking animals, birds, and insects aren't just for children. I found that many of Aesop's fables parallel, or at least reinforce, moral teachings of the Bible.

Aesop's history is sketchy. He was born a slave in 620 BC and eventually won his freedom by impressing his owner with his wit and wisdom. Today his name is attached to a whole class of ancient fables rediscovered during the Middle Ages and popularized about the time the King James Bible was published.

Let me share one of my favorites. In "The Kingdom of the Lion," Aesop tells of a lion that ruled forest and field. During his reign, the king of beasts assembled all of the birds and animals and presented his plan for a universal league of peace in which the wolf and the lamb, the panther and the goat, the tiger and the deer, would live together in perfect peace and harmony. Upon hearing the lion's decree, the rabbit said, "Oh, how I have longed to see this day, in which the weak shall take their place, without fear, by the side of the strong." Then the rabbit quickly ran for his life.

What Aesop Does for Us

He helps us think for ourselves. Because he doesn't do our thinking for us, Aesop's method of storytelling comes in under our moral and religious radar. Is he saying, "Don't trust your leaders. Government policy can't change human nature"? Could he be thinking, "Fearful people can ruin the noblest plans"? Or is he commenting on a prediction of the prophet Isaiah? In an earlier time and place, Isaiah wrote about a day when the wolf and the lamb would be at peace (Isaiah 11:1–9). Together, the Old and New Testaments of the Bible also speak of a coming world leader described as the Lion of Judah. Even if Aesop never heard of this lion or of a coming day when even wild animals will be at peace, his fable bears a striking resemblance to a teaching method of the Bible. Like the proverbs of Solomon and the parables of Jesus, he uses a simple but profound word picture to get access to our minds and to help us think for ourselves.

He helps us exercise our moral awareness. Aesop's writings work because all people, religious or not, have an inner moral awareness that regularly needs to be nudged and awakened. In the apostle Paul's New Testament letter to the Romans, he helps us understand why people who have never heard of the Bible can understand the wisdom of patience, the danger of pride, and the self-defeating nature of fearfulness, laziness, and cruelty (Romans 2:14–15). Because the laws of the Creator are written in our hearts, people like Aesop can illustrate and reinforce values and moral principles that are important to society and to the cultivation of personal conscience.

He helps us build. By putting words in the mouths of animals, Aesop may have unintentionally reinforced another theme of the Bible. People and animals have more in common than we may think. We owe our existence to the same Creator. We all live from the hand of God, and we are bound together by a complex interdependence.

Whether human or animal, Christian or Muslim, our lives are intertwined in ways that go far beyond our differences. Just as the cow and chicken feed us, the persons who deliver our mail or provide electric service might be Buddhist, Hindu, or atheist. None of us can afford to regard the other as being undeserving of our love and respect.

What Aesop Cannot Do for Us

Moralists and storytellers like Aesop can point to higher ground. They can help us think for ourselves. They can remind us to use our inner moral compass. And they can even help us build bridges to places we too-seldom go. But people like Aesop cannot do what Jesus did.

Aesop was a mortal like us. Jesus, in addition to being a perfect man, was God with us. Aesop cleverly reminds us of moral values. Jesus lifts morality to its ultimate implications and then rescues us from our rebellious condition and forgives our spiritual record.

Jesus did what no spiritual teacher or clever storyteller could ever do. He intervened in our moral dilemma, took our place on death row, accepted our punishment, and, as Judge of the universe, declares innocent all who trust Him. As the Lion of Judah, He invites us into His eternal kingdom where even wild animals will be at peace (Isaiah 11:6–9).

Jesus alone deserves our trust when He says, "Let not your heart be troubled; you believe in God, believe also in Me . . . I am the way, the truth, and the life. No one comes to the Father except through Me" (John 14:1, 6).

If you have never made a decision to accept Jesus as your personal Savior, Lord, and Teacher, I'd invite you to use this moment to pray something like this:

Father in heaven, I need the forgiveness and salvation that Your Son bought for me. I admit before You that I not only have sinned, but that, by nature, I am a sinner.

I also believe that Jesus is the only One who can bring me to You. I believe You loved us enough to send Him to our rescue. I believe He died on the cross to pay for our sins, and that on the third day He rose from the dead to be the living Savior of all who trust Him.

So now, from the depths of my heart, I accept His rescue. I take Him at His word when He says, "He who hears My word and believes in Him who sent Me has everlasting life, and shall not come into judgment, but has passed from death into life" (John 5:24).

Thank You, Father, for Your gift of salvation.

April 2007

Gender Issues

ARCHIE

ARCHIE BUNKER GOT LAUGHS in the 1970s as television's equal-opportunity bigot. But *All in the Family's* coast-to-coast laughs were more than entertainment. Archie's insensitivity to wife Edith, daughter Gloria, and the liberal son-in-law whom Archie called "Meathead" reflected years of profound social change. Society was rethinking men's and women's traditional roles.

Many of us laughed at Archie's antics, but some of us felt uneasy with the social changes going on. As the laughs died down, it was as if someone changed the channel and we were watching "The Friday Night Fights." In one corner was the Bible. In the other, a society awakened to principles of social and spiritual equality. On one wobbly knee in mid-ring was the traditional image of a husband and father. Going down for the count was the "sole provider" who used to come home, put up his feet, and read the newspaper while his wife prepared dinner and kept kids and dog off his lap.

As I reflect now on what's happened it's hard to believe how far both society and the church have come. A few decades ago male headship was assumed and many Bible-believing people said family leadership should be distinctively male. In many of our conservative churches, the Bible was preached as a basis for hierarchy. Authority was the law of the home. Husband was seen as the head of the wife, as Christ is head of the church (Ephesians 5:23). A wife was responsible to respect, submit, and obey. When there were problems that caused women to cry for help, they were often told to fix the problem by being more submissive.

So what changed? Why do many of us see family relationships differently? The answer is embarrassing. It's embarrassing that many of us in the church see marriage differently, not because we learned to study the Bible better but because our society slowly blinked, as if waking from a long sleep. And as eyes opened, church outsiders said women deserved respect.

Then came a ground swell of change, a new consensus. Women demanded rights and society agreed. Like dominoes falling, "the wave" of change gradually gave birth to a new day. Both outside and inside the church, it became clear: God made women as partners, not property. Men and women were made for mutual respect and love, not exploitation and control.

Suddenly, and to our amazement, the Bible seemed to agree. Old arguments for hierarchy sounded weaker now. Paul, it was discovered, didn't tell only wives to submit; he urged *all* Christians to submit to one another (Ephesians 5:21). Jesus, we were reminded, exposed the fallacies of self-centered male domination and headship. He said that real leaders are servants, and that the one who would lead must first become servant of all (Luke 22:25–27).

What happened to our biblical convictions? Does the Bible mean nothing? Or everything? Are the Scriptures chameleon-like, changing with cultures and contexts?

The challenge now is to recover confidence in Scripture. Worst case is to lose confidence in the Bible. Best case is to realize that while the Bible hasn't changed, circumstances like suffering, and failure, and social change allow us to change our focus on Scripture.

Is this new focus better or worse? Well, that depends on our answers to a few questions. Do we see more of the Scripture than we saw before? Does our new understanding encourage a more Christlike spirit? And when tested by those who disagree, are we convinced we're interpreting God's Word honestly and with respect for all the facts before us?

For centuries male spiritual leadership saw what was convenient to see. Today egalitarian culture sees what is equally convenient. Each generation is inclined to ride the pendulum to whatever extreme is in reaction to the previous generation's excesses and errors.

It's time for another look. We can't afford to forget what God's Word has always said: there's a leadership that's loving, and there's a thoughtful, honorable submission.

Marriage is difficult and complicated. But we can begin by acknowledging that husbands are responsible to God for taking wise, loving initiatives in the home. Wise husbands listen. Loving husbands care about the needs and thoughts of wife and family.

Wives need to educate themselves in the ways of God, and to thoughtfully walk with husbands who lead in a good and godly direction. Maybe this isn't the whole picture, but it's a place to begin again, and again, and again.

Equally clear is that we can't afford naiveté about married life's challenges. As a result of the Fall, God told Eve that the marriage relationship was damaged; it would be a fight for survival. Spiritually alienated husbands and wives now engage in a struggle for control (Genesis 3:16), despite vows to the contrary.

Father, forgive us for not taking Your warning or love seriously. Please forgive men and women for using our differences to control one another for our own sakes, rather than to love one another for Your sake.

March 1998

THE INVISIBLE WOMAN

I RECENTLY SAW A greeting card that shows a woman sitting in a business meeting with five men. The man at the head of the table says, "That's an excellent suggestion, Miss Triggs. Perhaps one of the men here would like to make it."

Men smile because the card catches them with their guard down. Women buy it because it validates their experience. A man repeats what a woman has already said, and others in the room act as if the thought has surfaced for the first time.

Who Is Miss Triggs?

She might be a staff member or a volunteer. She may know the organization inside out and do the work of several people. Informally, the men she works with depend on her knowledge and counsel. But when the time comes to make important decisions, she isn't taken seriously.

Miss Triggs is in a tough spot. She realizes that she is not being intentionally ignored, so she doesn't want to complain and be labeled a troublemaker. But it's difficult working and living on the blind side of men who can't see and don't appreciate her spiritual gifts. They see her carefully controlled and gracious demeanor without realizing that behind it is a woman who feels used and dismissed. She wants to be recognized for what she has to offer and included for the value of her contribution, but often she senses that men include her only so they can feel good about themselves.

What She Is Not Told

Women who are ignored or gradually shut out are rarely told directly that their opinions are not wanted or needed. Instead, they read between the lines and learn that they are expected to know their boundaries, to speak when asked, and to live as if God made men to think and women to work. No leader tells them that women are needed in the bedroom but not in the boardroom. Yet many women believe that this is what men really think.

The History of a Problem

The problem of men who watch women without seeing them has a history as old as the Bible. One especially provocative example shows up in the book of Esther. There we read about a self-absorbed king of Persia who threw a huge party and then ordered his wife to parade her beauty before his drunken guests. When Vashti refused to comply with her husband's command, it was as if she had drawn a line in the sand between all the men and women of the civilized world (Esther 1:15–22).

In an all-male "consultation," the king's advisors urged him to divorce and depose Vashti before her example caused all of the women of the kingdom to lose respect for their husbands. To make sure that every man remained master of his own house, the king sent letters throughout the kingdom declaring that because of Vashti's defiance, her royal position would be given to another (Esther 1:19, 22).

The book of Esther isn't just about women. It is about leaders who deny the humanity of those they see as a threat to their power and authority. To reinforce control of their homes and the kingdom, the king and his advisors got rid of Vashti. For similar reasons of power and control, the same king later was drawn into a conspiracy to destroy all of the Jewish people of the kingdom—because they bowed to a higher authority than the king of Persia.

A Different Kind of Leader

The Bible gives us another example of leadership. Jesus was also a king. But He wasn't like the king of Persia. He turned traditional notions of leadership and headship upside down when He said, "The kings of the Gentiles exercise lordship over them, and those who exercise authority over them are called 'benefactors.' But not so among you; on the contrary, he who is greatest among you, let him be as the younger, and he who governs as he who serves. For who is greater, he who sits at the table, or he who serves? Is it not he who sits at the table? Yet I am among you as the One who serves" (Luke 22:25–27).

The One who spoke these words was the Lord of lords. But He didn't walk with a swagger. He didn't ignore marginal people. Instead, He had a reputation of helping women, children, poor people, and even despised tax collectors to see their true importance.

A Better Vision

Because of the dramatically different example of Christ, He helps those who follow Him to see the difference between where we are and where we could be. The inconsistency itself can give birth to a dream of better relationships and healthier churches. In this vision:

❖ The values of Christ are seen in the way His people work and worship together. Because He knew the value of the person, those who lead in His behalf show the same regard for both men and women.

❖ People are more important than meetings. Relationships are more important than plans and budgets. And both men and women are given a chance to use their God-given gifts to make a difference in other people's lives.

❖ Men and women believe they can do together what both know they could not do by themselves. Both model their attitudes and behavior after the example of Christ.

❖ Elders do not lord it over the flock (1 Peter 5:1–3). Women are not treated like second-class church members. Both men and women take initiatives to plan their work, solve problems, and improve the quality of the services they are offering in the name of Christ.

❖ In these churches both men and women freely share ideas that are accepted or rejected not because of who expressed them but on the merits of the ideas themselves.

Although there is probably a considerable gap between this dream and our own reality, a vision of shared ministry is so worthy and uplifting that any degree of fulfillment will not only enhance our own lives but also the lives of those who still feel invisible.

Father in heaven, You have shown us a better way. Forgive us for being preoccupied with our own power and control. Please help us to give both

men and women the respect and honor that Your Son gave the Matthews,
Marys, and Marthas of His life.

March 2003

RULES FOR FAIR FIGHTING

ONE OF THE PROMISES OF marriage is that shared love will bring out the best in each other. I remember giving my wife Di an anniversary card that said, "I love you not only for who you are, but for who I am when I am with you."

But what happens when husbands and wives bring out "the worst" in their spouses? What can we do when we find ourselves using intimate knowledge of one another's weaknesses to do mutual harm? I ask these questions because Di and I have been there. In the falls and winters of our marriage, we have seen how difficult a best friend can be. We've found that no one can hurt us more than the one who knows us best.

Avoidance Strategies That Don't Work

As I recall, it didn't take long for us to discover that marriage is a two-way street where collisions happen with alarming frequency. Early on, I tried to apply defensive driving skills that work better on the road than in a relationship. I soon found that trying to avoid disagreements didn't resolve any of them. The tendency to want peace at all costs has been one of my biggest mistakes. I've learned the hard way that there is no way around the hard work of honestly talking through our differences.

Along the way, I also discovered that the Bible is better lived than quoted in an argument. Looking back, I can see that I've made the mistake of selectively quoting "submission" passages in self-centered attempts to get my own way.

Both Di and I have come to see that in times of disagreement we do better when we have made an effort to translate our knowledge of Scripture into the kind of practical wisdom that might be found in *Reader's Digest* or *Family Circle*.

Rules of Engagement That Do Help

We have noticed that it is usually more considerate to observe "rules for fair fighting" than to see "a husband's leadership" and "a wife's submission" as a God-given means of avoiding marital disagreements.

Along the way I've learned that much of the practical advice that shows up in the popular literature of the day is rooted in better spiritual principle than my initial attempts to assert marital headship. Consider, for instance, the following list. See if you agree that each rule could be a way of applying to marriage one of our Lord's most basic teachings: Do to others as you would have them do to you (Luke 6:31).

Rules for Fair Fighting in Marriage

* Agree that an issue is a problem whenever your spouse thinks it is.
* Give one another room for disagreement and the freedom to express a full range of honest feelings.
* Stay on the subject.
* Don't interrupt or "over-talk" in an effort to keep your spouse from saying what he or she wants to say.

- Preface comments with phrases like "I think," "It feels like," or "It seems to me" rather than declaring to your spouse what he or she is really thinking or trying to do.
- Avoid generalizations such as "You always" or "You never."
- Don't try to be judges of each other's character.
- Attack the problem, not each other.
- Don't argue at mealtimes.
- Don't use children or parents as weapons.
- Agree ahead of time to allow for a temporary "time out" if either of you becomes too angry to continue.
- Stay with a subject to a point of closure. If you can't resolve your differences, agree on how you are going to handle the disagreement.

This kind of practical advice can make a big difference in a marriage. The fact that it is not expressed in spiritual or biblical language may actually help us test our spiritual integrity. I've been around long enough to know that people of the church don't necessarily have better marriages than their unchurched neighbors. Sometimes we let our strong spiritual restraints against divorce become an excuse for carelessness. The law of marital permanence is often misused as a license for husbands and wives to take one another for granted. It's not enough to emphasize that marriage is "till death." We need to show that our marriages are marked by a love that others can understand and appreciate.

A Road That Can Be Walked in Two Directions.

Our Lord showed by His own teaching methods that there is benefit in moving back and forth between spiritual insight and natural wisdom. His parables repeatedly tapped the common sense of home, business, and nature. In most cases He appealed to observations that were secular rather than religious in origin.

By religious standards, some of His examples were even scandalous. On one occasion He used an unethical businessman to show that sometimes unbelievers are more shrewd at reaching their goals than believers (Luke 16:1–9). In another lesson He made a hero out of a man (a Samaritan) whom his religious audience would have considered spiritually unclean (Luke 10:30–37). Over and over Jesus used the behavior of outsiders to help His religious listeners see what they were missing.

We too can be humbled and helped by the "Samaritans" of our day. They may not share our spiritual beliefs, but they can usually recognize a healthy marriage when they see one.

An Admission That Renews My Faith

Subjecting our spiritual principles to a "secular road test" has been important to Di and me. More than any other relationship, our marriage has made us aware of our personal need of Christ's forgiveness, teaching, and renewing presence in us. Nothing has given me more pain—or more joy.

And I have a hunch that the kind of renewal Di and I have experienced is what others are looking for. I'd bet a paycheck (knowing I wasn't risking a dollar) that when the principles of Christ are applied to the details of marriage, the results look like the kind of mutual love and respect the whole world longs for.

August 2002

A FIRE

A FIRE IS SMOLDERING IN many of our homes, offices, and hearts. Those touched by its flames are left with scars of self-contempt, distance in relationships, aversion to God, and diminished ability to help others. The fire is pornography.

In the past, sexually explicit material was available only in out-of-the-way places. It is now as accessible as the Internet. In the privacy of our own homes or workplaces, anyone can access not only research libraries, up-to-the-minute news, and e-mail, but everything that used to be limited by social boundaries.

Why is this happening? Why are some of our best men giving in to the temptation? In part because all of us, like Elijah and Samson, are troubled by our own passions (James 5:17). We are all subject to feelings of loneliness, rejection, anger, and foolishness. We all crave intimacy in relationships, and pornography provides a powerful, thoughtless illusion of that intimacy.

Let's see if we can see why the alarm needs to be sounded.

It is not just a male problem. While men are the primary users of pornography, both men and women are hurt. Pornography damages everyone. It sexualizes otherwise innocent relationships and fills minds with secrecy and dishonor that will not be left in the closet.

A man might think he can cross sexual boundaries and then lock up his failures in a secret compartment of his life. But secrets of the heart live close to everything else that is important to us (Proverbs 4:23). A loss of conscience results in a loss of transparency, and, as a result, a loss of intimacy.

It destroys our capacity for intimacy. Seeing women as objects of self-centered pleasure has a dehumanizing effect that blinds us to their pain and happiness. It blurs the image of God which together we share. It preoccupies us in a cycle of self-absorbed pleasure, regret, shame, and concealment. The pride that makes us afraid to admit our own failures leaves us with a sense of self-contempt that fills us with ourselves, rather than with the interests, thoughts, feelings, and needs of others.

It sets up a god-substitute in our heart. It is impossible to keep a healthy focus on the Spirit of God and His Word while assuming that the rancid food of pornography is the bread we need and want. It is just as impossible to walk in the Spirit when walking under the influence of our own flesh. When full of ourselves, we are not under the influence of the Spirit (Galatians 5:16).

It defaces a place of worship. We would not think of defacing a house of worship. Yet for those who have taken the name of Christ, choosing the illusion and god-substitute of pornography is like writing obscenities on church walls. Our bodies are a temple (1 Corinthians 6:19). Images burned into the mind cannot be painted over. A man who sacrifices his soul for pleasure diminishes his capacity for good and for God. He lives with a conscience that directs him away from God rather than toward Him.

It costs more than we think. Self-centered pleasure lasts for a moment. Memories and regrets can live for a lifetime. Though our Lord is quick to forgive when we come to Him with honest hearts, His mercy does not automatically fix a damaged thought-life nor patterns of deceitfulness.

The fire of pornography leaves us with a coolness toward heaven and earth. It puts distance between ourselves and others. It robs us of our conscience before God and our transparency with others.

It requires more than a casual response. Those caught in the grip of pornography cannot fix the problem by simply turning over a new leaf or by renewing personal resolve. As with other enslaving sins, we need a sustained, thoughtful approach to the implications of our choices. We need to do whatever it takes to unmask the wounded pride that is keeping us from seeking help. We need to thoughtfully look for the desires and thoughts of the Lord. Where is He? What is He saying? What is He feeling? What is He offering?

Then we need to ask Him for the ability to look deep into ourselves, to see not only what we are doing to ourselves and others, but why. What are the lies we are telling ourselves? What are the misbeliefs? We need to call upon the Lord for the forgiveness and enablement He alone can give.

We also need to find a friend or professional who will strengthen our resolve. When the Scriptures tell us to confess our faults to one another, they are not giving us a substitute for confession to God. Neither are they allowing us to think that confession to God is all we need. Honest, appropriate accountability is one way to build boundaries and restraint back into our lives.

Father, thank You for calling us to the higher ground of Your love and to the level ground of the cross. Thank You for urging us to clean house, to develop mutual respect for one another, and to have a healthy view of the sexuality You have given us. Forgive us for forgetting that You have linked our sexual desires to the multiplication of Your image, and thereby to the most important issues of our life. Separate us to Yourself, and lift us from any bondage that has made it difficult for us to honor You—and to love one another. Remind us of the words of Your servant who said, "The Lord knows those who are His," and "Let every one who names the name of Christ depart from iniquity" (2 Timothy 2:19).

September 1997

AN ARGUMENT

DIANE AND I HAVE BEEN married for thirty-one years. For more than three decades it seems as if we've been talking, laughing, and disagreeing about almost everything. My reason for mentioning the disagreements is that I've been thinking again about one issue we've found especially difficult. Time after time we've argued about the way women are treated in our circles. Having served on church elder boards, I've repeatedly argued that most of the men I've known are doing the best they know how to do. Di insists that all too often the good that men are trying to do doesn't reflect an understanding of the needs of women.

Roots of a Disagreement

There is a history to Di's concern. She has been deeply involved in domestic crisis issues in our church and community. As a result, she often sees women and children hurt by men who not only know the Scriptures, but who also use the Scriptures to demand unreasonable kinds of submission and silence. Di regularly reminds me of ways men use the biblical principles of headship and submission to multiply the pain of women and children.

In response, I've reminded Di of the progress we've made. I've assured her that along with a lot of other men, I've realized that headship gives husbands the authority to serve their wives, not lord it over them.

A Problem of Credibility

The progress that reassures me, however, is another thing that troubles Di. Along with a lot of other women, Di is struggling to understand why men are suddenly talking about servant leadership and sacrificial headship. Why has it taken so long to see that principles of submission and love must be offered voluntarily rather than coerced from one another? What does such an obvious oversight in the past say about our ability to see clearly on other issues now?

Seeing the Light

Di has been right more often than I want to admit. As a woman, wife, and mother, she understands better than I do how women are hurting. She has helped me to see how much damage is done when the Scriptures are misused to shape relationships by power and authority rather than by love and respect. In the process, I think I've developed a deeper awareness for how careful I need to be in applying the Scriptures to the relationships of men and women.

Handle the Scriptures Like a Loaded Gun

"Safety first" is the rule for firearms. Always treat a gun as if it is loaded. Be careful where you point even an unloaded gun. Whenever you shoot, know what is behind your target. Don't risk unintentional injury or death.

The Scriptures deserve to be treated with as much care as a loaded gun. The Word of God is dangerous in the hands of people who use biblical principles to get their way. A man who wounds a woman's spirit by using the Bible like a club or a gun is not using the Word of God for its intended purposes. He is promoting a heresy of misapplication.

Handle the Scriptures Like Prescription Medicine

Prescription medications are ordered by a doctor for a specific person with a particular problem, and they're to be taken in a definite manner for a certain length of time.

The Word of God is like prescription medication. It is to be administered with an understanding of where love and truth are missing. It is to be offered carefully in the right manner to the right person. Forgiveness, headship, submission, comfort, peace, reconciliation, and restoration are all meant to be thoughtfully and carefully applied in the Spirit of Christ. When they are forced down the throats of others, in an effort to get our own way, we risk choking the spiritual life out of the one we are trying to control.

Handle the Scriptures Like a Timepiece

An analog watch cannot be taken apart and put back together without great care. Every part must be put in its right place. Gears designed to work together will not work apart from their original design.

In a similar way, the Word of God is meant to work according to the design of the Spirit of Christ. Headship and submission were not intended to help husbands dominate or control their wives. Repentance and forgiveness were not meant to guarantee restoration-on-demand to offenders. Each principle has a God-given time and place. We can't afford to misplace any piece. All were meant to work together to provide help rather than harm in the family of God.

Handle the Scriptures Like Seed

Seed in a farmer's barn is valuable because it contains the future harvest. But before it will bear fruit, the seed has to be planted at the right time in specially prepared soil. In order to germinate and grow to maturity, seed requires the right amount of water, seasonable temperatures, and time.

The Word of God requires similar attention. Knowledge alone will not change a life. In fact, the accumulation of biblical knowledge can lead to arrogance and legalism (1 Corinthians 8:1). If planted in a cluttered heart, the seed of the Scriptures will shrivel and die (Luke 8:5–8). Even though a person knows enough Bible to sound authoritative, the result can be to use the Scriptures like the devil, rather than like Christ (Matthew 4:1–10).

Forgive me, Father, for using Your Word for my own purposes rather than Yours. Forgive us for hurting Your reputation by using Your words to hurt those who need our love. Help us to have the kind of hearts that give others reason to trust You.

April 2000

HEADSHIP

WHAT THE ALL-MALE ADVISORS of King Ahasuerus feared has happened (Esther 1:10–22). Wives in growing numbers are rejecting the idea that a man should be the head of his home.

The reaction was inevitable. Too many husbands have tried to prove their masculinity by demanding obedience from their wives.

More than a few of us have felt justified in doing whatever it takes to assert our headship. Some have threatened and even battered their wives into submission. For just as long, many have misused the Bible to feed the problem. Abusive husbands and well-intentioned counselors have quoted 1 Peter 3 to tell even endangered wives that if only they would be more submissive, their husbands would have no reason to mistreat them.

Until recently, the rule of submission has so eclipsed a husband's responsibility to love that many of us have not been able to see when the principle of submission no longer applies. Even though we have honored David for running from the violent authority of King Saul, we have urged women to be more submissive (rather than less) to the distorted authority of angry, abusive husbands. We have been blind to the fact that just as David honored Saul while separating from him (1 Samuel 24:6), so an endangered wife can continue to honor (and even love) her husband while taking steps to remove herself and her children from his violence. Today many are finally understanding that the Scriptures say far more to battered women than 1 Peter 3. Read 1 Corinthians 7:10–11, Matthew 18:15–17, and 1 Samuel 25.

But now the pendulum is swinging back. The better part of a generation now has concluded that mutual love and submission are the whole picture of Christian marriage. We've forgotten that Ephesians 5:22–33 is in our Bible.

I'm part of the problem. On too many occasions I missed the point of my headship in marriage. Rather than loving my wife as Christ loved the church, I focused on her "responsibility" to submit. I conveniently forgot that the kind of leadership Jesus called for is to be "as one who serves" (Luke 22:25–27).

Christlike headship does not give a man the right to yell at his wife, threaten her, or hit her. Neither does a husband's headship require a woman to be mindlessly passive in the face of her husband's pride. What a husband's loving leadership does do is give a woman reason to be thankful for the difference Christ can make.

Does this mean a husband has to be Christlike before a wife has to acknowledge that submission is more than a two-way street? No. But it does mean that those of us who claim to be Christian husbands need to focus on our own responsibility to love—unselfishly and sacrificially—rather than on our wives' responsibility to submit.

November 1995

MARITAL ABUSE

MARITAL ABUSE COMES HOME when it happens to someone we care about. Imagine if the following were your daughter:

A Woman in Pain

She doesn't know where to turn and blames herself for ending up in an abusive marriage.

You know your daughter isn't perfect. But what you haven't seen is how often she's cried, and how hard she's tried to make her marriage work. For the last twelve years she has prayed that God would give her the patience and grace to stay with the man she promised to love for the rest of her life.

Sometimes, however, she wishes she had never been born. Her husband tells her he doesn't love her and says he's sorry he married her. He calls her names, deprives her of affection, and yet, whenever he's in the mood, expects her to meet his sexual demands. When she talks about getting help, he threatens to tell her friends that she's mentally ill or that she's having an affair. She doesn't doubt that he would lie to protect himself. He leaves bruises and deep wounds others cannot see.

When your daughter has confided in church leaders, they have advised her to be more submissive and not to criticize him or provoke his anger. They usually ask if he has been sexually unfaithful, but she doesn't think he has. Some have asked if she thinks he's really a "believer." She tells them, "He says he is." When she asked one elder why those questions were important, he told her that without sexual unfaithfulness or the abandonment by an unbelieving spouse, she doesn't have biblical grounds to leave her husband. The same church leaders have told her that separation is not an option because it is often the first step to a divorce.*

Tough Questions

The subject of marital cruelty opens a Pandora's box of questions. If we allow separation and open the door to divorce, how many marriages will be lost? How can we know that a woman is not merely looking for an excuse out of an unhappy marriage? On the other hand, does a "no-divorce-for-abuse policy" honor the purpose of marriage?

Often-Overlooked Answers

Just as Genesis reveals God's original intent for marriage, Exodus and Deuteronomy show principles of marital justice in a fallen world.

Moses did more than describe God's sacred purpose for marriage. He also wrote laws granting protective divorce to the most powerless and socially disadvantaged women in Israel. Even for daughters who were sold into slavery to satisfy a family's financial debt (Exodus 21:7–11), and for foreign women

---

* This description of the private world many women are enduring is excerpted from *God's Protection of Women* by Herb Vander Lugt (Discovery Series, RBC Ministries).

captured as spoils of war (Deuteronomy 21:10–14), Moses decided against the husband who did not honor the most basic terms of the marriage covenant.

In another law, Moses allowed a husband to divorce his wife with only one surprising stipulation: he could not marry her again if she was divorced or widowed from another man in the meantime (Deuteronomy 24:1–4). In a legal system severe enough to require the death penalty for those who committed adultery, Moses did not forbid divorce or remarriage.

These laws are like "the other side of the coin" to foundational values of home and family. While recognizing that marital permanence is God's ideal, Moses also recognized that hard-hearted conditions can be worse than divorce.

The question facing us is whether or not we should allow the wisdom of the Old Testament to inform the way we deal with severe marital abuse in the church today.

Jesus and Paul both emphasized marital permanence. Neither spoke, as Moses did, about protective divorce for abuse.

So what are we to make of their silence? Do Jesus and Paul leave behind principles of marital justice? No. When Paul writes that all Scripture is inspired by God and full of wisdom for life (2 Timothy 3:16), his words remind us that the Old Testament was the first Bible of Jesus and the apostles. Even though the Law was fulfilled in Jesus, and even though the form of the Law passed away, timeless principles like mercy, justice, and concern for the downtrodden are affirmed throughout the New Testament (Matthew 23:23).

When we take Paul's advice and consider the whole counsel of God, we find an interesting relationship between divorce and Sabbath law. At first glance, we might wonder if both are parts of the Law that are no longer in force. On further consideration, however, it becomes evident that what is important about both is their timeless intent. Neither come into the church age as binding law. Both, however, move forward as timeless principles that reflect the care of God for His people.

Consider the following incident as an illustration of how important it is to understand not only the words of the Law but its heart and spirit.

According to the gospel of Luke, Jesus went into a synagogue on the Sabbath and healed a woman who had been bent over for eighteen years. When the ruler of the synagogue saw what Jesus had done, he was angry because Jesus had violated the no-work policy of Sabbath law. Jesus, however, showed that it was the leader of the synagogue who misunderstood the heart and spirit of the law (Luke 13:10–16). In a similar incident, Jesus later asked, "Which of you, having a donkey or an ox that has fallen into a pit, will not immediately pull him out on the Sabbath day?" (Luke 14:5).

When someone we love is struggling with severe marital abuse, it is not difficult to see the connection between her situation and that of the woman bent over before Jesus on the Sabbath day. When someone we care about is in severe pain, we begin to see the importance of a Christlike response that takes into consideration the timeless intent of God's laws.

And so we pray, Father in heaven, please give us the wisdom and mercy of Your Son. Please help us to honor Your purpose of marital permanence, while being able to show Your care and wisdom to those who need help.

March 2006

DIMINISHED CAPACITY

IN AN AGE OF EQUAL RIGHTS, it is sometimes difficult to see the Bible as a friend of women. Although some texts treat husbands and wives as equals (1 Corinthians 7:4), other passages view women as the "weaker vessel" (1 Peter 3:7) and place them in a supporting role rather than a leading role (Ephesians 5:22–25).

In another time and place, the Bible's approach to gender looked different. In a patriarchal world, daughters and wives were viewed as property. In such a setting the Scriptures elevated the status of women.

Today, however, the suggestion that a woman should submit seems backward and even un-American. What if a wife has better judgment than her husband? What if she is more gifted in making and managing money, hanging wallpaper, or fixing things around the house?

Conditions of Diminished Capacity

As a rule, we don't question a woman's leadership if her husband loses his ability to protect and provide for his family. Few will criticize a wife for stepping up to the challenge if her husband is: physically disabled; diagnosed with a debilitating mental or emotional condition; or morally entangled in an addiction that blinds him to the needs of his family.

Some, however, have missed the extent to which such lost capacity is a significant factor in the Bible's approach to men and women.

The History of Diminished Capacity

The first pages of the Bible describe the origin and results of impaired judgment. At the onset of human mortality, God Himself declared that weeds and thorns would sprout from the earth, pain would complicate childbirth, and men would rule their wives (Genesis 3:16–19).

Although most of us work to minimize the curse of weeds in our yards and the pain in childbirth, some of us have not seen the subordination of women as part of the same curse. As a result, we have seen male dominance as a principle to affirm rather than a problem to be minimized. Yet the Bible itself shows that in circumstances of diminished capacity, God is flexible in His approach to the complementing roles of men and women.

Abraham is widely regarded as "the father of us all" (Romans 4:16). His legacy is rich in faith but also includes impaired reason and flawed judgment. In several examples of diminished capacity, both he and his wife Sarah made the mistake of following one another's advice (Genesis 12:11–20; 16:1–4). Along the way, however, Abraham learned that it is not beneath a man to submit to an imperfect woman. In a difficult family dispute, the Lord told Abraham to defer to Sarah's demands (Genesis 21:9–12).

Abigail is an example of a woman married to a man whose pride blinded his judgment. Rather than submitting to her husband's stubbornness, she protected her family by providing care and assistance to David and his hungry soldiers (1 Samuel 25).

Then there is Deborah, who rose above the prominence of her husband in ancient Israel, acted as a judge in matters of social dispute, and in a moment of national crisis led the army into battle (Judges 4–5).

The Example and Teaching of Jesus

No one, however, gives us a better example of how to respond to conditions of diminished capacity than Christ Himself. In heaven He was "with God" and "was God" (John 1:1). In the presence of His Father, angels obeyed His every word. Yet He willingly and lovingly stepped into history to become the Servant of servants and the Husband of a very imperfect and unfaithful church.

No one had more right to be followed. No one had more inherent ability to rule. Yet in the words of Paul, Jesus "made Himself of no reputation, taking the form of a bondservant, and coming in the likeness of men. And being found in appearance as a man, He humbled Himself and became obedient to the point of death, even the death of the cross" (Philippians 2:7–8).

Christ's self-limitation and submission were voluntary. His example was intentional. To His disciples Jesus said, "The kings of the Gentiles exercise lordship over them, and those who exercise authority over them are called 'benefactors.' But not so among you; on the contrary, he who is greatest among you, let him be as the younger, and he who governs as he who serves. For who is greater, he who sits at the table, or he who serves? Is it not he who sits at the table? Yet I am among you as the One who serves" (Luke 22:25–27).

Capacity and Love-based Leadership

Christlike leadership, whether expressed by a man or a woman, involves caring for others with the abilities and circumstances that God has given. Any physical strength or social opportunity is to be used to protect, provide, and complement, not to control and to dominate.

On the other hand, wise persons recognize their own gifts and limitations. They know that love and truth are more important than authority or roles. They find joy in discovering that the grace of a Christ-like attitude can make any strength or weakness a showcase for the presence and sufficiency of God (2 Corinthians 3:5).

The apostle Peter wrote, "As each one has received a gift, minister it to one another, as good stewards of the manifold grace of God . . . that in all things God may be glorified through Jesus Christ, to whom belong the glory and the dominion forever and ever" (1 Peter 4:10–11).

The sovereign power that Peter referred to blends in mysterious ways with the unfairness and inequities of our fallen, broken world. Men often end up with physical and social advantage. Sometimes, especially in our technologically developed world, the pattern is reversed. In the long run, what counts is whether we use the capacities God has entrusted to us to seek the honor and well-being of those who need our help. What matters is whether we work with our Lord, or against Him.

Father in heaven, we see in You a heart that is so different from our own natural inclinations. Our impulse is to control and to use. Yours is to care and to love. Our focus is on our own immediate desires. Yours is the well-being of others. Please let the Spirit and mind of Christ be what others see in us today.

April 2004

Things That Are to Come

THE RETURN OF CHRIST

ONLY HOURS BEFORE HIS DEATH, a carpenter rabbi from Nazareth told His followers that He was leaving them. Then He said, "Let not your heart be troubled . . . I will come again and receive you to Myself; that where I am, there you may be also" (John 14:1–3).

Almost two thousand years later, many are still waiting for the fulfillment of that promise. In 1992, pollster George Barna reported that seven out of ten Americans believed Jesus would return at some time in the future. In 1997, an Associated Press survey showed that 24 percent of American adults believed Christ would come back in their lifetime.

A Legacy

My grandfather, founder of RBC Ministries, was one who lived with the daily anticipation of Christ's return. Until his homegoing in 1965, he viewed the national rebirth of Israel, the growing influence of the United Nations, and the emergence of atheistic Russia as indicators that the Bible's predictions about the last days were coming to pass. Then, for two decades after his passing, my father Richard continued to teach the any-moment return of Christ. Today, Dad's body is buried near his own father's memorial stone that says, "Perhaps Today."

Changing Conditions

In the last few decades world conditions have changed dramatically. The breakup of the Soviet Union, an uneventful turn of millenniums, a series of false alarms sounded by well-publicized date-setters, and the surprising popularity of the *Left Behind* novels have all influenced the way we think about prophecy. In addition, several recent books have been written to challenge the "maybe today" view of Christ's return.

What Christ Said about His Return

Many students of the Bible believe Jesus never told His disciples to think of His coming as imminent. As evidence, they point to passages such as John 21:18, which says that Jesus told Peter not to expect Him to come back before Peter was an old man. Furthermore, in a private conversation with His disciples, Jesus told them that His return would follow unprecedented events: "The sun will be darkened, and the moon will not give its light; the stars will fall from heaven, and the powers of the heavens will be shaken" (Matthew 24:29). Then, according to Christ, He and His angels will come with an unmistakable display of power (Matthew 24:30).

Something Else Christ Said

It's important to know, however, that Christ also included an element of mystery about the time of His coming. To keep us ready and watching, Christ said other things that don't seem to fit His promise to return on the heels of the worst trouble the world has ever known. On other occasions He told stories illustrating the importance of being ready for His return, adding, "for the Son of Man is coming at an hour you do not expect" (Luke 12:40).

How could both be true? How could our Lord say to His disciples that He would come at a time they didn't expect if His coming will be preceded by the signs described in Matthew 24:21–30?

A Precedent

This is not the first time the people of God have been faced with prophecies that seemed contradictory. The ancient rabbis of Israel could not understand why their prophets talked mysteriously about a coming Messiah who would be both a suffering servant and ruling king. They didn't know that these two distinct roles of Messiah would be fulfilled by two comings separated by at least two thousand years.

An Implied Parallel

Our situation today may be similar to that faced by Old Testament Jewish people. We too have pieces of a prophetic puzzle that don't seem to match. The difference today is that God has given us a precedent for expecting more than one appearance. We now have reason to consider a scenario which, though not explicit in the text, seems to be implied. If there are yet two more parts to Christ's return, His coming could be both imminent (any moment) and several years away (after the sun and moon are darkened with judgment).

But why would two more appearances be necessary? One answer involves the similar but distinct nature of Israel, and that international body known as the church.

A Reason for Two More Appearances

Israel and the church are similar in that both share the same spiritual heritage. Both are loved by the same God. Both are grounded in the scrolls of Jewish prophets. Both are a "chosen people," called to be a light to the nations.

But there are also broad and far-reaching differences. Israel is a national body founded on the teachings of Moses and focused on a land, a temple, a priesthood, and the promise of a Messiah who will subdue and rule the earth (Isaiah 2:1–4). The church is an international body, a living temple made not of stone but of people, all of whom are priests and messengers of God. They've been sent out into the world to represent the mind and heart of Christ until He returns to lead them, and the friends they've made, back to His Father's house (John 14:1–3; 1 Thessalonians 4:15–17).

These similar but distinct roles of Israel and the church give us a reason why Christ might speak in such different terms about His return. Because Israel and the church have similar but distinct relationships to God, we can see why our Lord's coming to remove the church from the world could be imminent, while His return to rule the world will happen only after the sun and moon stop shining.

An Unchanged Expectation

The most important facts have not changed. Regardless of changing international conditions, we still have our Lord's promise to His disciples: "Let not your heart be troubled . . . I will come again and receive you to Myself; that where I am, there you may be also" (John 14:1–3).

We also still have the mystery. We have every reason to live as if His coming could be a moment away, just as we have every reason to plan for the future as if His coming will not happen in our lifetime. For almost two thousand years the watchword has been, "Maybe today. Maybe not."

January 2003

A PREDICTION

ONE OF THE MOST AMAZING predictions of the Bible was made in the middle of a national disaster.

The pride of Israel had been broken. On the heels of a military defeat, some of the most religious people in the world wondered if God had abandoned them. Many of Israel's brightest and best young people had been exiled to Babylon, a region known today as the nation of Iraq.

One of those young men was an exile named Daniel. In the dark shadows of Babylon he developed a reputation for interpreting dreams and predicting the future.

Today we look back at Daniel as an important Jewish prophet who not only deepened the anticipation of a coming Messiah, but also predicted *when* this Messiah would come. This prediction is so provocative that many scholars have tried to argue that the prophecy at the center of the controversy must have been written after the fact.

In 1948, however, ancient copies of Daniel were found in the Dead Sea Scrolls. Scholars were forced to admit that Daniel's predictions were written no later than the second century BC.

That conclusion places the prophecies well before the events that were predicted.

So what did Daniel foresee? He said the long-awaited Jewish Messiah would come before the destruction of a rebuilt temple. Even more specifically, the prophet said Messiah would come after a period of sixty-nine "sevens." This is the kind of prophecy that deserves front-page coverage on every newspaper of the world.

What is the background of this prophecy?

Seventy sevens of history—While in exile, Daniel learned why his nation had been defeated in the Babylonian invasions of 605 and 586 BC. By studying the prophet Jeremiah (Jeremiah 25:11; Daniel 9:2), he discovered that his people were enduring seventy years of exile for 490 years of spiritual neglect. During that period they showed their disregard for God by failing to give their fields seventy seventh-year Sabbath rests.

Seventy sevens of future—As Daniel looked back over 490 years of spiritual idolatry and unfaithfulness, he learned that his generation was at a pivotal point in history. According to chapter 9 of his prophecy, the angel Gabriel appeared to him and revealed that another period of "seventy sevens" would pass before God's Messiah appeared to bring the peace they had been waiting for (Daniel 9:24–27; Isaiah 2:1–4; Genesis 12:1–3).

The Prediction Was Messianic in Scope

Some Jewish writers insist that the Messiah foreseen in Daniel's vision was the Persian King Cyrus who conquered Babylon and then gave the Jewish people permission to return to their homeland. They point to the prophet Isaiah who quotes God as referring to Cyrus as "My anointed servant" (literally "my messiah") in Isaiah 45:1.

Cyrus was God's chosen servant to return Israel to her land. But Cyrus doesn't fit the rest of the picture (see Daniel 9:24). Daniel's Messiah was to come sixty-nine "sevens" after the "edict of return." Then this Messiah was to be "cut off," as if in defeat, prior to the long-anticipated peace of a messianic age (v. 24).

The Prediction Says When Messiah Would Come

As we look back, Daniel's prediction was that Messiah would come sixty-nine sevens (69 x 7 = 483) after "the issuing of the decree to restore and rebuild Jerusalem" (Daniel 9:25 NIV). When was that command given? There are three possibilities. The Bible mentions three edicts of two Persian kings who gave the Jewish people a right of return to their homeland. In 539 BC, Cyrus issued a decree allowing the Jewish people to begin rebuilding their temple. Artaxerxes later issued two decrees. His first in 458 BC also authorized the rebuilding of the temple. His second in 444 BC clearly allowed restoration of both the temple and the city of Jerusalem.

To see the amazing significance of this prophecy, look what happens if we test the possibility that Daniel was foreseeing 483 (69 x 7) *years* rather than 483 days or months. If we begin in 538 BC and follow Daniel's prediction of sixty-nine sevens, we come to about 55 BC. If we begin at 458 BC we come to AD 25. And if we begin at 444 BC and move forward 483 years we come to about AD 38.

What is so compelling to me is that adding 483 *years* to any of these start dates leads to a time-frame that is close, but prior, to the destruction of Jerusalem in AD 70. If Daniel was predicting 483 periods of time greater than *years,* the result would go beyond the AD 70 destruction of Jerusalem.

The Prediction Says Messiah Would Be "Cut Off"

Even though Jesus of Nazareth lived within the time frame that Daniel seems to anticipate, many Jewish people insist that Jesus could not have been the true Messiah because He did not bring in the expected kingdom of God. Yet Daniel, along with other Jewish prophets, indicates that the Messiah of Israel would be "cut off" (i.e., killed) in apparent defeat before reigning as King of kings (Daniel 9:26; Isaiah 53:1–8, 10–12; Zechariah 12:10; 14:3–9).

The prophecy shows that the "anointed one" would be "cut off" *after* the 69th "seven," and prior to the resumption of the 70th (Daniel 9:26–27).

Do you see the implications of this? Daniel gave us not only a time-frame for when the Messiah would come, but he also told us that this "anointed one" would be rejected before bringing the peace of His kingdom to earth.

Who Could This Messiah Be?

Who within Daniel's time frame could qualify as the "cut off" Messiah? And if the crucified and resurrected Jesus is the only one who qualifies, who can afford to ignore Him? If Christ alone is God's promised Savior and King, where—but to Him—can we turn for forgiveness and immortality?

If He came the first time, as predicted, we have every reason to hear His promise to return at a time known only to God. Our Lord says, "Be ready, for the Son of Man is coming at an hour you do not expect" (Matthew 24:44).

May 2005

FUTURES TRADING

THE WALL STREET WE SEE on the evening news looks out of control. The flailing arms and white shirts on the floor of the trading pit give the appearance of a madhouse way of doing business.

The Earlier Chaos

The confusion, however, is more orderly than the system it replaced. Before the development of "futures contracts," farmers hauled their crops to town looking for buyers. In years of a big harvest, when supply exceeded demand, an abundance of grain or corn drove the market down to give-away prices. Grain often rotted in the streets or was dumped in the river. A few months later, spring shortages could push prices on corn- or grain-based products so high that only the wealthy could afford them.

The Development of Futures Trading

In the mid-19th century, central grain markets developed a system of futures contracts that allowed buyers and sellers to do business at today's prices for commodities that would be delivered in the future. Commercial hedgers, who were trying to limit their risk of loss, began to do business with market speculators, who were willing to take risks in search of profits. The animated buying and selling we see on the evening news is a snapshot of floor brokers trying to get a high price for their sellers and a low price for their buyers.

The Bigger Picture

In the past I've looked at the world of Wall Street from a distance. When aggressive phone marketers called about a hot investment opportunity, I'd say, "Sorry, I'm not in the market."

What I've since realized is that, by reason of living, we all are "in the market." In the clamor of daily life, each of us trades for or against the future by the decisions we make today. Most of these investments have nothing to do with commodities or a stock exchange. They are decisions of the heart needing the advice not of E. F. Hutton but of the most published investment book in the world.

Ironically, as familiar as we might be with the Bible, its rules of "futures trading" are more likely to be misunderstood than the white shirts and trading pits of Wall Street. Consider, for instance, how the following principles of spiritual investment run counter to conventional wisdom.

Live Beyond Your Means

Living in the moment can push us to spend more than we make. One of my favorite lines comes from "The Lockhorns" newspaper comic series. "Sure, I spend more than you make," Loretta says to husband Leroy. "I have confidence in you."

Although living beyond our means is a danger sign for personal finance, it is essential for spiritual investment. Jesus saw the advantage of those who knew their need for help when He said, "Blessed are the poor in spirit, for theirs is the kingdom of heaven" (Matthew 5:3).

If Jesus was right, the most enviable people in the world are not those with more money than they can spend. Real wealth belongs to those who are willing to live on the name and credit of One who has the resources to pay their way now and forever.

Don't Hedge Your Bets

In the world of finance, one thing is certain. Markets will change. The value of stocks and commodities are in a continual state of flux. Money managers, therefore, try to limit risk by hedging investments. They put some of a client's money on a rising economy and some on a fall.

Although caution in financial investment says, "Don't put all your eggs in one basket," the rule for spiritual trades is just the opposite. The God of the Bible will not reward those who have a strategy of spiritual diversification. While teaching His followers how to "lay up treasures in heaven," Jesus said, "No one can serve two masters; for either he will hate the one and love the other, or else he will be loyal to the one and despise the other. You cannot serve God and mammon" (Matthew 6:19–20, 24).

Don't Try to Be Too Practical

Many have observed that even if there were no God, no heaven, and no hell, it still would make sense to live an honest life and to treat others the way we want to be treated.

Jesus, however, takes a different view. Without denying the benefits of living well, He reminds us that practical people can cash out too soon. He said that if someone practices their religion for the affirmation of others, then, in the applause, they already have their reward (Matthew 6:2, 5, 16).

Emphasizing the eternal value of deferred rewards, Jesus counseled His followers to give secretly to needy people, to pray in secret, and to exercise spiritual discipline in secret. Waive public notice, Jesus suggested, "And your Father who sees in secret will reward you" (Matthew 6:1–6, 16–18).

Without denying the possibility of immediate benefits, Jesus saw the greater potential of future rewards. In contrast to the depreciating investments of this world, the Teacher said, "Do not lay up for yourselves treasures on earth . . . but lay up for yourselves treasures in heaven . . . For where your treasure is, there your heart will be also" (Matthew 6:19–21).

Don't Worry Away Your Profits

While teaching His disciples to trade for the future, Jesus repeatedly told them not to worry about the basic material needs of life (Matthew 6:25, 28, 31, 34). But why did He emphasize the avoidance of worry as a way of putting stock in heaven?

Many of Jesus' first disciples paid a great price to follow Him. Thousands lost the security of jobs, homes, and family. It was only natural for them to wonder how they were going to provide for themselves and their families while on the run. Jesus probably warned against anxiety for another reason as well. Those who are worrying are not trusting. And without trust there is no investment in the future. Because faith is more precious than gold in God's sight, anything motivated by faith in what He has said is like a direct deposit in the bank of heaven (1 Peter 1:7). By the same logic, any lack of faith is lost opportunity.

Father in heaven, for the joy that was yet ahead, Your Son traded His life for ours. Please help us to spend the rest of our days investing in the future You have bought for us.

December 2005

HELL

I WISH I DIDN'T HAVE to believe in hell.

While seeing the need for eternal justice, the thought of cruel and unusual punishment that lasts forever sounds morally wrong to me. Yet the Bible describes God as a great King who creates a lake of everlasting fire for rebels who want no part of His kingdom.

As a child, I thought of hell as being like the agony of falling into a real fire. More than fifty years later, I'm trying to believe no more and no less than what the Bible requires us to believe.

I've thought a lot about the story Jesus told of a callous rich man who died and found himself in Hades. Even before the final judgment, the man was suffering in flame and torment (Luke 16:19–31). Whether Jesus was speaking in a parable or not, I've found some solace in the fact that the man in the fire was able to carry on a conversation. He was not suffering in the way I imagined as a child.

Admittedly, Jesus didn't tell the story to comfort us. He went on to describe how the man in the flame asked for a messenger to be sent back to the land of the living. He wanted his five brothers to be warned about this place of torment. But he was told, "If they do not hear Moses and the prophets, neither will they be persuaded though one rise from the dead" (Luke 16:31).

The end of Jesus' story raises a question. What did Moses and the prophets say that amounted to fair warning?

Hell in the Old Testament

Moses describes the Lord of heaven as the judge of all the earth. Like the New Testament that follows, he even describes God as a consuming fire of judgment (Deuteronomy 4:24; 9:3; Hebrews 12:29). Together with the rest of the prophets, he warns about the dangers of death and "the grave." Beyond such warnings, however, the Hebrew Scriptures say little if anything about suffering after death. Daniel gives the most specific information when he predicts, "Many of those who sleep in the dust of the earth shall awake, some to everlasting life, some to shame *and* everlasting contempt" (Daniel 12:2).

In a specific example of judgment, Isaiah uses the language of unquenchable fire to describe the fate of those who die on the battlefield at the end of the age. Speaking in apocalyptic language, the prophet says, "For their worm does not die, and their fire is not quenched. They shall be an abhorrence to all flesh" (Isaiah 66:24). The revulsion Isaiah speaks of has a physical setting. It occurs as living people look on the dead bodies of those who have fallen under the judgment of God. A Jewish reader in Isaiah's day would probably not have seen anything in these words about conscious suffering after death.

Hell in the Teachings of Jesus

In some versions of the New Testament, "hell" is a translation of the Greek word *Gehenna*, a place known in Old Testament times as the Valley of Hinnom. Jesus uses a word picture of the garbage dump to the south of Jerusalem where the refuse of the city was burned. Jesus uses this real place of burning rubble to illustrate the fate of those who gain the world but lose their soul (Matthew 16:26).

On several occasions Jesus speaks of the wailing and gnashing of teeth that will accompany final judgment (Matthew 13:42). Three times in Mark 9, He draws on the words of Isaiah when He describes the danger of "the fire that shall never be quenched—where 'their worm does not die.' " If Jesus uses these words in the same way as Isaiah, He is warning about the horror of divine judgment without telling us for how long or to what degree such persons suffer.

Hell in Revelation

The language of "eternal conscious torment" comes most clearly from the last book of the New Testament. In a book that uses strong symbolic language to sound clear warnings of judgment, we read that all those who worship the beast (Revelation 14:11), the beast himself, the false prophet, and the devil will all be cast into the lake of fire where "they will be tormented day and night forever and ever" (Revelation 20:10). Chapter 20 goes on to say that Death, Hades, and everyone not found written in the Book of Life also will be cast into the lake of fire (Revelation 20:14–15).

So how do we take these warnings to heart without losing our minds over lost loved ones? Our challenge is to believe as Abraham did, that "the Judge of all the earth [will] do right" (Genesis 18:25). Such a God understands infinitely better than we do how to exercise justice that is consistent with His own character.

Degrees of Punishment

Jesus repeatedly indicated that judgment will be more tolerable for some than for others (Matthew 10:15; 11:22, 24; Luke 12:46–48).

In addition, Revelation 20:15 does not explicitly say that everyone who is cast into the lake of fire will suffer in the same way as the devil and those who worship him (Revelation 14:11; 20:10). Trying to read between the lines ignores the principle that "The secret things belong to the LORD our God, but those things which are revealed belong to us and to our children" (Deuteronomy 29:29).

For what we cannot understand, those of us who bear heartache for lost loved ones need to trust the One who loves them far more than we do. He has told us as much as He wants us to know. The rest we need to leave in His hands.

Father in heaven, forgive us for saying more or less than You have revealed. Thank You for assuring us that You take no delight in the death of those who reject You (Ezekiel 33:11). Help us to lovingly warn those who still have an opportunity to accept Your mercy. And when we are overwhelmed with concern, please help us to remember that everything You do in judgment is right, and necessary, and good.

November 2006

RESCUE

IN THE SUMMER OF 2002, a coal mining accident left nine Pennsylvania men trapped 240 feet underground. For three days the men huddled in the darkness of a cramped space that had filled almost to the top with 55-degree water.

On the surface, a nation watched as rescue efforts dragged on longer than expected. Broken drill bits hampered attempts to dig an escape shaft through solid rock. Finally, after three long days and nights, rescuers broke through to the air pocket below. A few minutes of confusion followed. Then three emotion-filled words spread through the crowd of waiting families and neighbors: "They're all alive."

Upward Thoughts

The odds were beat that day. Prayers were answered. A feared outcome was dodged. A mining community added to its memories a story that CNN.com remembers as "The Quecreek Miracle."

It's natural in a crisis for even secular people to have God on their lips. We don't have to see angels to know there is more to life than what we can see. Our own experience anticipates what the Bible confirms. Whether seen or not, there is a connection to all human experience. Any goodness echoes of God. Any happiness is a hint of heaven. Any danger reflects the greatest danger. Any rescue foreshadows the ultimate deliverance predicted in the last words of the Bible.

For some of us, it may be a stretch to connect the dots between the moments of our lives and the "last days" predictions of the Bible. But, if Jesus can be trusted, there is a real link between His offer of "daily bread" now and ultimate rescue later. The same Lord who offers, in the Gospels, to walk with us in our daily needs, ends the book of Revelation with the promise, "'Surely I am coming quickly.' Amen. Even so, come, Lord Jesus! The grace of our Lord Jesus Christ be with you all. Amen" (Revelation 22:20–21). These are the last words of the Bible.

If this doesn't sound like the type of Savior we need to survive the concerns of today and the apocalyptic culminations of the last days, we don't understand the scope of our need.

Downward Inclinations

From Genesis to Revelation, the Bible tells the stories of people who think they can go it on their own, until something brings them to the end of themselves. Only then are they likely to admit that, to their own loss, they have been ignoring the One who is offering them strength for the day and hope for the future.

The "chosen people" we meet in the pages of the Bible are a mirror of our own tendency to be our own worst enemy. Throughout their history, the people of Israel have been inclined to focus on the threat of their natural enemies. What their prophets repeatedly told them, however, was that the threat of war, weather, or disease was not nearly as dangerous as their own inclination to turn their backs on God whenever a crisis had passed.

Because we need Him in good times as well as in bad, the Scriptures urge us to focus all of our lives on the One who has promised, "Surely, I am coming quickly."

Forward Thinking

Christ may come today. Or He may come tomorrow or one hundred years from now. But that's His decision, not ours. Our part is to make sure that if He does come today, He will find us doing His business rather than our own.

Doing His work means looking for His return, but not waiting. It means living with an expanded anticipation of possibilities.

Maybe today we will find the grace of Christ to be better than the relief we are seeking. The apostle Paul repeatedly asked the Lord to remove an unnamed "thorn in the flesh" (2 Corinthians 12:7). But when the problem remained, Paul surrendered to God's presence in the pain. He discovered that he would rather experience God's strength in his weakness than to have no problem and no sense of how desperately he needed the enabling grace of his Lord.

Maybe today we will have an opportunity to bring the rescue of Christ to someone in need. This is the high purpose of God. All who have discovered the love of Christ have been called to care for others as He has given Himself for us. Our call is to work together with Him as His hands and feet to the needy and lonely people in our lives. The challenge is not merely to wait, but to keep on praying, working, and watching, in the spirit and purpose of our Lord.

Maybe today we will see our Lord rescue us through physical death. Because we don't know if Christ will return in our lifetime, we need to be realistic about our own mortality. While the will to live is a gift of our Creator, we must also come to terms with a willingness to die in Christ, if that is the will of our God. Only by being ready to meet Him in life or in death can we find the courage to live without an obsession with self-protection and fear.

Maybe today Christ will come. This is the hope that re-emerges once we have our eyes refocused on the ultimate rescue of Christ.

So, Father in heaven, please help us to live with the highest of hopes today. We are not proud of the fact that we are inclined to look only for the satisfactions of the moment. For all of the good pleasures of life, we are thankful. But please help us to look for opportunities to be Your hands and feet to those who need to join us in being ready for the One who said, "Surely I am coming quickly."

January 2006

PITFALLS OF PROPHECY

NO GENERATION HAS EDGED as close as ours to the end of the age. Who can deny that the world is looking more and more like the Bible's description of the last days. Even secular thinkers are aware of Armageddon-like possibilities. And now, at this late date, I'm having second thoughts about how we've handled our views on the future.

I'm not doubting that prediction of the future is a major emphasis of the Bible. One-third of the Scriptures are prophetic in nature. Jesus Himself emphasized the importance of prophecy when He said, "Be ready, for the Son of Man is coming at an hour you do not expect" (Matthew 24:44).

Yet, almost two thousand years later, the church is deeply divided over what Jesus meant by the time of His return. Many have read and embraced the popular *Left Behind* series, which describes fictional scenarios on earth following the return of Christ for His church. Others believe that the prophetic view of this series is more fiction than fact.

In an unavoidable way, I have inherited a place in the prophetic fray. My grandfather, Dr. M. R. De Haan, founder of

RBC Ministries, was known for his impassioned teaching of the premillennial, pretribulational return of Christ. He considered a knowledge of the prophetic Scriptures to be a powerful incentive for his listeners and readers to get ready for the any-moment "rapture" of the church.

There were reasons for my grandfather's passion. He believed that the Bible's predictions about the last days will come to pass just as literally as those prophecies of Scripture that have already been fulfilled. He saw the 1948 restoration of Israel as evidence that prophecy must be taken at face value. Because he saw a restored nation of Israel as part of the Bible's description of the last days, he was convinced that Christ would return within his lifetime (1891–1965). He lived by the motto "Perhaps Today."

Almost forty years have passed since my grandfather's home-going. Since his death, failed expectations together with intense disagreements over scenarios of the future have divided the church. All of this has prompted me to take yet another look at how we hold our prophetic views.

The Dangers of Prophetic Study

1. Using prophetic convictions as a test of faith. In line with the legacy of my grandfather, I remain convinced that Christ could return at any moment. I believe His return will come in two phases: first as Head and Savior of the church; then, at least seven years later, as the King and Savior of Israel. But at this late moment in time, I've become even more sure that I need to respect those who have come to different conclusions about the last days.

I've grown increasingly certain that it is wrong to doubt the faith or the faithfulness of those who believe that the church will pass through all or part of the tribulation; that the church has permanently replaced the nation of Israel in God's plans for the future; or that Christ's return will not result in a literal thousand-year reign on earth.

2. **Using current events to tell "prophetic time."** I have little doubt that the rebirth of Israel and the trends toward globalization are setting the stage for the return of Christ. But in the middle of such anticipation I am equally convinced that we need to avoid the temptation to connect current events with the fulfillment of specific prophecies.

Few actions have contributed more to the demise of prophetic teaching than the exaggerations or miscalculations of those who assumed they understood the prophetic countdown.

The Importance of Prophetic Study

1. **Using prophecy to keep the faith.** Prophecy reminds us that God is great enough to allow genuine human freedom while remaining in control of the outcome. No one knows how He does it—but, at the very minimum, God is like a great chessmaster who allows the moves of human choice while remaining in control of the board. He will finish what He started. God's final moves have already been determined. We may break His heart, but no one will break His will or frustrate His plan.

2. **Using prophecy to keep hope alive.** In the past, people like Simeon and Anna found that enduring hope in the promises of God were a source of great joy, even if they died before the future resurrection (Luke 2:34, 36).

The prophecies of the Bible continue to give hope to those who believe them. The predictions of Scripture remind us that history is on schedule. We are not all passengers on a runaway bus. Through resurrection or "translation" we will all arrive at our chosen destination (1 Thessalonians 4:15–17).

Our challenge is to keep hope alive without being foolish or presumptuous. Wisdom will teach us to say of Christ's return, "Maybe today. Maybe not." We need to be ready to go with Jesus now, or to stay here awhile longer. We need to teach our children to join us in looking for Christ's return while also preparing for the possibility of a long and full life on earth.

3. Using prophecy to help us love one another. In writing to those who had entrusted themselves to Christ, the apostle Paul praised them for working hard as they waited for the return of Christ. He affirmed not only their "work of faith" and "patience of hope," but also their "labor of love" (1 Thessalonians 1:1–10). Paul's logic is understandable. Just as anticipation of an "imminent" visit from the corporate office puts workers on their best behavior, so a healthy expectation of Christ's "any-moment" return teaches His people to reflect the values and virtues of their Lord.

Father, please forgive us for acting as if the present will never end. Too often we have sacrificed our future on the altar of impulse. Sometimes we've been willfully ignorant of what You want us to know. Sometimes we've been stubbornly proud of the little bit we've learned. Please help us to love one another in the light of all that You've said will happen in Your time—not ours.

April 2001

FISHING

I LIKE TO FISH. No, I *love* to fish. I love fishing so much that sometimes it becomes an obsession. Sometimes fishing is way too important to me. But why? A lot of the time I catch nothing. On occasion all I come home with is a story of the one that got away: the big smallmouth that broke my fly rod, or the steelhead that jumped and thrashed its way to freedom, or the monster carp that did whatever he wanted with my line until spitting out the hook.

So how can I, in a world of things that really matter, stand or sit for five hours when the fish aren't biting and still enjoy it? What is so great about stepping into the boat, cranking up my 15-horse Evinrude, and heading for a good underwater drop-off or promising weed bed? Why is it that if the water is calm, the sun is getting low, and I can hear bluegills kissing bugs in the lily pads, that I succumb to the illusion that all is well with the world?

There is something about the natural drug of expectation. Anticipation. Hope. Imagination. Thinking about what might happen on the next cast, the next retrieve, the next move. As much as I love a good lake or river, I wouldn't go fishing if I *knew* I wasn't going to catch anything.

The best thing about fishing, though, is that by thinking about it I've rediscovered a desire to live my whole life with anticipation. What could be better, as the sun begins to set on these last days of time, than to work the edge of an unseen future with the hope of catching a moment of faith, an act of unselfish love, or of genuine hope in God! What could be better than to hunt for an opportunity to be obedient and submissive to the Spirit of God! What could be more challenging than to probe the unseen world of the Spirit, looking for a chance to show self-control, to resist temptation, to choose good rather than evil, to know and agree with God, to experience His grace, to experience His power, to suffer with Him, to rejoice with Him, to endure with Him!

What could make a better day than to capture an opportunity to show undeserved kindness and Christlikeness, to endure difficulty with grace, to show joy in testing, to discover wisdom, to hunger for rightness, to fear God, to trust Him, to believe in Him, to listen before answering, to encourage a troubled person, to follow through on a promise, to pray for someone, to prepare for hard times, to have a good conscience, to speak with grace—to know Christ.

Father, teach us to live with expectation. Help us to live in anticipation of Your Son's any-moment return. As the sun of this age gets lower in the sky, enable us to be in pursuit of that which will be worth talking about for all eternity. Help us to hear Your Son who said, "Come, follow Me, and I will make you fishers of men" (Matthew 4:19 NIV).

May 1995

NOTE TO THE READER

The publisher invites you to share your response to the message of this book by writing Discovery House Publishers, P.O. Box 3566, Grand Rapids, MI 49501, U.S.A. For information about other Discovery House books, music, videos, or DVDs, contact us at the same address or call 1-800-653-8333. Find us on the Internet at http://www.dhp.org/ or send e-mail to books@dhp.org.